Israel: Politics, Myths and Iden

Pluto Middle Eastern Series

General Editor: **Uri Davies,** University of Durham and
University of Exeter

Israel Shahak, *Jewish History, Jewish Religion*

Israel: Politics, Myths and Identity Crises

Akiva Orr

Pluto Press

LONDON · BOULDER, COLORADO

First published 1994 by Pluto Press
345 Archway Road, London N6 5AA
and 5500 Central Avenue
Boulder, Colorado 80301, USA

94 95 96 97 98 5 4 3 2 1

British Library Cataloguing in Publication Data
A catalogue record for this book is available from the British
Library

Library of Congress Cataloging in Publication Data
Orr, Akiva
    Israel: politics, myths, and identity crises / Akiva Orr.
    170p. 22cm. – (Pluto Middle Eastern series)
    Includes bibliographical references and index.
    ISBN 0-7453-0766-3
    1. Israel. 2. Zionism – Controversial literature. 3 Jews –
Identity. 4. Jewish–Arab relations – 1949– I. Title. II. Series.
DS102.95.077 1994
320.5'4'095694 – dc20   94–2269
                                                            CIP

Designed and produced for Pluto Press by
Chase Production Services, Chipping Norton, OX7 5QR
Typeset from disk by Stanford DTP Services, Milton Keynes
Printed in Finland by WSOY

Contents

Acknowledgements

Thanks are due to Roger van Zwanenberg of Pluto Press for publishing this book.

To Dr Uri Davies for promoting it to the publisher.

To Deborah Weil for turning a collection of articles into a book.

To Christine Considine for her meticulous editing work.

The author is grateful to Zmora-Bitan, publishers, for permission to reproduce extracts from 'Khirbet Khiseh' by Yzhar Smilansky.

The publisher would be interested to hear from any copyright holders not here acknowledged.

Other Books by the Author

Peace, Peace, and No Peace, with M. Machover, Hebrew, Israel, 1962

The unJewish State, Ithaca Press, London, 1983

Introduction

This book consists of various essays dealing with the politics and ideology of Zionism, the sociology of Israel and politics of ethnicity generally. Some of these essays were written during the past 20 years, some are new. Each essay is self-contained, dealing with a particular issue and is fully understandable without reference to others. Yet they all have one thing in common: they comprise an anthropocentric critique of ethnocentric politics and ideology.

No-one can observe society (or nature) from an objective viewpoint although many fall for this illusion. Any observation is made by a subject and is based on assumptions. These assumptions flow from a particular ontology and a particular value system. Striving for clarity requires that the author of a critique state explicitly the value system which guides the critique. In social affairs there are only four possibilities: egocentrism, theocentrism, ethnocentrism, and anthropocentrism. My standpoint is anthropocentric. This is where I stand, though, unlike Luther, I could stand elsewhere. Luther thought he couldn't choose otherwise; we know we can. We can choose to be egocentric, like most people in the West today, or ethnocentric like many in Eastern Europe, Asia or Africa. We know that value systems are acquired and can be changed. They cannot be imposed but can be accepted unconsciously.

May these essays motivate the reader to explore her/his value system.

To the memory of
Mordechai Stein and Jabra Nikola
who struggled for a society
without discrimination, oppression, exploitation.

Part One

IDENTITY

Introduction: Jewish Identity

The essays in this section deal with issues of group-identity which have motivated the political activity of many Jews in the past century. In the first essays I try to explain that the term 'Jew' is inseparable from a particular religious practice. Many people who consider themselves Jewish will object to this assertion. I refer them to my book: *The unJewish State* published by Ithaca Press (London, 1983). Any person insisting on being 'Jewish' yet not practising the religion has problems of defining his/her Jewishness. Private, personal, definitions abound, and they may satisfy the particular person, but none is generally accepted as binding for all 'Jews', and usually scrutiny will reveal that there is nothing specifically Jewish about that definition. The inability to produce a secular definition of Jewishness was a driving force of Zionist activity. The secular Jewish state was to provide the source of secular Jewish identity. However, in the state which Zionism created, a new, unexpected, ethnic identity emerged, namely that of Israeliness. The Israeli is 'a Hebrew-speaking gentile'. This is not the 'New Jew' which secular Zionism aspired to create but an anathema to Zionists and to most Jews outside Israel. So far a conspiracy of silence has surrounded this subject. May these essays contribute to an airing of the issue.

1

Motives for Writing a Book on Jewish Identity

In 1983 Ithaca Press in London published my book entitled *The unJewish State*. How did a lazy person like me ever come to write a book like *The unJewish State*, which took me seven years of archive research and three years of writing (for which I didn't get a penny) on a subject outside my profession?

The answer lies in two incidents that occurred while I was in England.

In 1967 I lived for a few months in Golders Green, a London borough with a large Jewish middle-class population. My landlord was an 80-year-old German Jew who had emigrated to England after Hitler had come to power in Germany. He was neither Orthodox nor Zionist. He used to go to the synagogue on Jewish holidays for traditional reasons. In other words, although he was a non-believer, he felt himself Jewish and found it necessary, psychologically, to attend religious ceremonies, like the fast on Yom Kippur, or the Passover meal (Seder).

When the tension between Israel and Egypt rose early in June 1967, a few days before it erupted into war, my landlord met me on the porch as I returned from university. Usually our verbal exchanges were restricted to 'Lovely weather, isn't it?', 'Hope it lasts', etc. This time, however, he asked me: 'What do you think, Mr Orr, will they destroy us?'

This stopped me in my tracks. What the hell did he mean by 'us'?

He lived in England, never visited Israel, had no relatives there, yet spoke like someone about to be attacked personally. I intended to point out to him that, after all, the Egyptian army did not muster at Calais and was not about to invade Britain and attack him in Golders Green. But as I looked at him it suddenly hit me that he was utterly sincere. He really felt as if he was about to be attacked. It was then that I suddenly understood what Israel meant to a certain group of Jews (who are neither Orthodox nor assimilationists, and wish to maintain their Jewishness without resorting to religion). To such people the state of Israel serves as a psychological prop for their sense of identity. It enables them to overcome the lack of clarity – caused by their loss of belief – of their Jewishness.

4

When Jews cease to live daily life according to Jewish religious rules, their sense of Jewishness immediately becomes blurred. They find themselves haunted by an insecurity whenever Jewish identity is concerned. This insecurity is experienced as a threat. The cause of this threat is externalised. They interpret every comment and joke about Jews as anti-Jewish racism. The state of Israel serves as a prop to overcome this insecurity. Jews in such a situation have a psychological need for Israel (the 'solution' to their 'roots' problem), unlike Orthodox or assimilationist Jews who focus their identity on God or on the host society.

All this flashed through my mind in a split second as I contemplated my reply to my landlord. I suddenly found the missing piece in a puzzle I had tried to solve for years – namely, why did so many British Jews react so emotionally whenever I criticised Israel? After all, I was an Israeli citizen, they were not; I served in the Israeli army in 1948, they did not; I studied and knew the history and politics of Israel inside out, they did not; what right did they have to react so hysterically to my criticism of my government?

My landlord's 'us' made it clear in a flash. He, like all non-religious, non-assimilationist Jews, embedded Israel in his identity. Any criticism of Israel was experienced by him as a criticism of himself. And any attack on Israel, be it verbal or military, was experienced as an attack on himself. Just as a religious person would be outraged at criticism of God, so are these ex-Jews outraged whenever anyone criticises Israel. In both cases an external entity is embedded in the structure of personal identity. Any critique of that entity is taken as personal.

Of course I didn't tell my landlord all this. I calmed him down by saying that whether or not a war broke out Israel would not be destroyed by it.

The second incident occurred in 1970, when I was speaking in Scarborough at a fringe meeting of the Liberal Party annual conference. I explained that the conflict between Israel and the Arab world was essentially a conflict over lands and independence between Jewish immigrants and the indigenous Palestinian population. Until 1948 Palestine was populated by an Arab majority which was expropriated, exploited, and partially expelled by the Zionist immigrants from Europe. The immigrant settlers transformed the indigenous majority into a minority discriminated against in its own country, and imposed upon it a discriminatory state apparatus, namely a 'Jewish state'. No wonder the natives were restless. This came as a total revelation to the audience of some 500, who were used to apologetic versions of the Palestine conflict, in which Israel was presented as a small, democratic state created by the Jews who escaped from Auschwitz, a state that made 'the desert bloom', and that was beleaguered by the surrounding Arab states for the sheer fact that it was Jewish.

A lively session of questions from the audience followed. Suddenly someone at the back of the hall stood up and shouted, emotionally: 'Israel expelled the Palestinian Arabs in 1948 as a response to the Jews who were expelled from the Arab states. This amounted to a "population transfer", which had occurred more than once this century and was a legitimate, if cruel, way of settling minority problems.' I replied that in 1948 Jews were not expelled from countries like Iraq, Morocco, Algeria, Tunisia and Lybia, but induced to leave by Zionist emissaries from Israel who often used dirty tricks like throwing bombs into synagogues to create the impression of anti-Jewish persecution to stampede the Jews to Israel.

This answer outraged my heckler even more, and he shouted in an agitated voice: 'You are a liar, no Jew ever threw a bomb into a Jewish synagogue.' The audience weren't used to seeing someone denounce a speaker as a 'liar'. Being British, they assumed such an accusation was based on solid information capable of withstanding a libel charge. The ball was now in my court, but having encountered this charge many times before I was well prepared. I had copies of the Israeli weekly *Haolam – Ha-zeh* (of 20 April and 1 June 1966) with me, which published details, with photographs, of these events. Some Iraqi Jews who had become disabled as a result of the bombs thrown by Israeli agents into the Mas-uda Shemtov Synagogue in Baghdad had sued the Israeli government for damages, in Israel. The government had preferred to settle out of court and pay damages, but the legal exchanges had reached the Israeli press and had been published by some magazines. When I read out the details of the case from the Israeli magazine all eyes turned back towards my adversary. I demonstrated convincingly that I was not a liar. What would he say now?

There was a moment of silence and then he blurted out: 'You see, unlike the Arab countries Israel is a democratic state. You can publish everything in the press there.' The audience burst into laughter; I didn't. This answer illuminated the tortured mental landscape of the non-religious, non-assimilationist Jew. This person had to defend Israel by hook or by crook. In fact he wasn't defending Israel, he was defending his self-image from his own conscience. Like my landlord in London who felt under attack, personally, by the Egyptian army in 1967, so did my heckler feel criticised, personally, by any criticism of Israel, especially one coming from an Israeli, which therefore could not be written off as anti-Semitic (the usual substitute is the concept of 'self-hating' Jew).

These two incidents revealed to me the psychological background of the Jewish support for Israel – whatever atrocities it commits –

by all those non-religious, non-assimilationist Jews. Identification with Israel helped them shore up their diffused notion of Jewishness. They didn't know that in Israeli law the notion of secular Jewishness is even shakier than their own, because the term 'Jew' appears in Israeli law, and requires a legally valid definition that the non-religious majority is unable to provide. I therefore decided to explore the history of the legal attempts in Israeli law to provide a secular definition of Jewishness in order to explain to those troubled Jews that Israel cannot provide a solution to their insecurity. I summarised my findings in my book *The UnJewish State*.

I knew that no one else would write that book. Leftist critics of Israel would consider all this stuff too airy-fairy – they can handle motives like economic exploitation, but cannot see how an insecure sense of ethnic identity can act as a powerful motivation in politics. Non-Jews are blinded by the Holocaust from seeing a process of cultural disintegration which has nothing to do with the Holocaust. Orthodox and assimilationist Jews find the issue irrelevant, whereas for Zionists it is too dangerous to discuss. An unbiased exploration of the issue reveals that Zionism is primarily an attempt to provide a political solution to an ethnic identity problem. Yet no state can be a substitute for a faith. An identity based on a faith will vanish when the faith vanishes, and no state can fill that gap. The religious definition of 'Jew' in Israeli secular law reveals the failure to provide the desired solution.

2

The Fragmentation of 'Jewish Identity'[1]

In March 1990 the Union of Jewish Students in the UK (UJS) published a 36-page pamphlet entitled *RETURN: Jews and Jew-Haters*. The pamphlet was directed against the first two issues (March 1989 and March 1990) of the magazine *RETURN*. The articles in *RETURN* were critical of Zionist policies; most were written by Israeli and British Jews.

The UJS pamphlet claimed that any critique of Zionism is a critique of Jewishness, and therefore racist. It accused the authors of *RETURN* of being racist Jew-haters. The President of the National Union of Students in the UK (NUS) accepted these accusations and banned *RETURN* from the NUS Conference.

Are the accusations valid? This raises three questions:
What is the nature of Jewishness (or 'Jewish identity')?
What is the nature of Zionism?
What is the relation between these two?
These questions have a cultural as well as political dimension. As the controversy between the UJS and *RETURN* was primarily political, the anthropological aspects of the problem were largely overlooked. A political analysis of a cultural problem tends to obscure the cultural issues. This essay deals with the 'Jewish identity' problem primarily from a point of view of cultural anthropology.

The Original Jewish Cultural Identity

Cultural identity is group identity. It is the manner in which a group defines itself. Cultural identity is not defined by individuals or outsiders. Individuals can define their own identity, not the group's. If they use the name of the group's identity for their private definitions they are misleading themselves and others. Outsiders can describe a group, persecute it, try to exterminate it; they cannot provide a self-definition.

For some 2,000 years Jews had a very clear, unambiguous and uncontested self-definition of their group identity: 'Jewish identity' meant the practice of religious rules for the conduct of life. These rules are known as mitzvot (religious injunctions), a derivative of the Hebrew word tzav (injunction). 'Jewish identity' consisted of practising the mitzvot daily. Anyone who practised them daily was known to himself and to others as a Jew. No one has ever challenged the assertion: those who practise the mitzvot are Jews. This is the only definition of 'Jewish identity' which has never been challenged by anyone. It is unchallengeable. There is not a single example of a person who practised the mitzvot and was a non-Jew.

This definition is not the official religious one (which is a circular definition, based on the mother's 'Jewish identity'). It is an anthropological one put forward by the author of this essay. All other definitions of Jewishness – including religious ones – have been challenged, are challenged, and lack general acceptance.

Let us consider some aspects of the mitzvot. It is not easy to practise the mitzvot. They are a burden. They make life much more difficult. They are a burden because they affect many mundane activities, but those who practise them accept this burden willingly and bear 'the yoke of Torah (holy scripture) and mitzvot' as a sacred duty. They denounce those who 'reject the yoke of Torah and mitzvot' as renegades.

The mitzvot determine not only when and how to conduct religious worship, but also what one is allowed – or forbidden – to eat (for example, various animals are forbidden; anything milky must be totally separated from anything meaty, separate sets of dishes being required for each; no milky dish may be eaten within two to six hours of a meaty one). The mitzvot also rule on what one is allowed to wear (for example, cloth which mixes animal fibres with vegetable fibres is forbidden). They rule when one is allowed to have sexual relations, how to wear one's hair and clothing, etc. In short, the mitzvot prescribe not only worship but also the practice of ordinary, daily, life. The mitzvot transform ordinary life into a religious way of life. If you wash your hands out of respect for God rather than for your own hygiene, you impart a religious meaning to that mundane act.

In short, those who practise the mitzvot experience much of their daily life as an act of worship. Worship is not confined to a particular place or time; it is practised also by means of everyday acts of daily life. Those who practise the mitzvot, and there are still many of them today, have no urge to 'define' their own identity. They never ask themselves whether they are Jewish and what is the meaning of their Jewishness. They experience their identity by practising the mitzvot. They have a totally secure cultural identity, known to themselves and to others as Jewish.

Jewish communities have, like many others, an initiation ceremony. Any initiation ceremony introduces the adolescent publicly to full membership of the community. It transforms the adolescent from a member of the family to a member of the community and imposes on him/her the community's code of behaviour and its duties. The particular elements of an initiation ceremony display what that particular community considers to be unique to itself, thus defining itself. The initiation ceremony is the manifestation of a community's self-definition.

The Jewish initiation ceremony is entitled 'bar mitzvah', that is, 'capable of obeying a religious injunction' ('mitzvah' is the singular of 'mitzvot'). This title alone already indicates that performing the mitzvot is what every Jewish community considered for millenniae to be its definitive quality. The bar mitzvah ceremony is still practised today even by non-religious Jews, when their sons reach the age of 13. None of these non-religious people ponders on the meaning of the title of this ceremony. No alternative title has ever been proposed by those who seek alternative definitions of Jewishness.

The fact that the Jewish initiation ceremony asserts, by title and content, that the daily practise of the mitzvot is the definition of Jewishness is proclaimed by the Jewish communities themselves – by all of them, whether in Yemen or in Poland, in Spain or in Persia, in the past or in the present. There is not a single example of a Jewish community anywhere, any time, conducting an initiation ceremony with a different name or content.

A further argument for recognising the practice of the mitzvot as the definitive feature of 'Jewish identity' is the empirical observation that during 2,000 years of Jewish history any group or individual who ceased to practise the mitzvot disappeared from Jewish history without leaving their mark on it. Some of these groups maintained themselves as 'Jews' for a few generations according to their alternative definitions of Jewishness, but eventually they disappeared from Jewish history without succeeding in propagating their notion of Jewishness. In other words: the practice of the mitzvot was more than a definition of Jewishness. It was – for 2,000 years – the only definition of Jewishness.

This last point is where the controversy over the definition of Jewish cultural identity starts. Those who practise the mitzvot insist that theirs is the only valid definition, and all other definitions are subterfuges of people who reject the genuine substance – and burden – of 'Jewish identity'. Those who do not practise the mitzvot – yet insist on defining themselves as Jews despite this fact – argue that there are other valid definitions of 'Jewish identity'. The controversy is over the validity and content of the other definitions.

Problems of Alternative Definitions of Cultural Identity

Since the early nineteenth century increasing numbers of Jews have ceased to practise the mitzvot; today they constitute about 80 per cent of the Jewish people. Many of them actually violate the mitzvot when they 'work' on Saturdays (for example, when they drive a car, switch on a light, or light a fire), or eat seafood, or drink coffee with milk after a meal in which they have had some meat, or when they marry non-Jews. Many of these people consider themselves Jews. However, the meaning of this term becomes blurred. From a religious point of view, they are still Jews, but sinners. These sinners are divided into two groups: assimilationists and adaptationists.

The assimilationists do not insist on being 'Jews'. They are willing to give up their Jewishness altogether and assimilate into the societies in which they live. They don't mind marrying a non-Jewish partner. They may be puzzled by their Jewish background. Those who don't insist on remaining Jews do not have a 'Jewish identity' problem.

Some assimilationists insist that they are still Jews, and do have an identity problem. Many residues of Jewish tradition evoke nostalgia in assimilationists and are still practised by them, but without the original conviction. In general, it takes a few generations for assimilation to succeed. The assimilationist may suffer from anxiety about 'roots', but this diminishes from one generation to the next.

The adaptationists have a problem which does not diminish with time. Adaptationists wish to adapt 'Jewish identity' to the modern world. They insist that they are Jews, despite the fact that they do not practise the original mitzvot. They produce new definitions of the mitzvot, relaxing the severity of some and abolishing others. There is no reason to doubt that they feel Jewish, but when asked to clarify what their Jewishness means they will give a variety of different, often conflicting, answers. They have no generally agreed definition of 'Jewish identity'. Their definitions often suit non-Jews. Whatever their own definition, they have to admit that the practice of the mitzvot is a valid definition.

Adaptationists have a legitimacy problem because their definitions are in conflict with the original definition and with each other. The three adaptationist groups, Reform, Conservative, and Reconstructionist, are constantly struggling against the insistence of the Orthodox Jews (who adhere to the original mitzvot) that their own definitions have no validity. They all admit that 'one who practises the mitzvot is a Jew', but claim validity also for their own relaxed versions of the mitzvot. However, their own versions – three different ones – cause constant controversy.

Before discussing the problems of alternative definitions of Jewish cultural identity, let us consider some difficulties of alternative definitions of cultural identities in general:

- Use of the same label to denote different substances is bound to cause confusion.

- There is an asymmetry between the status of the original and the new definitions; if the original use of a label is still in force, any alternative use has an inferior status. It lacks the legitimacy of the original. In the domain of commerce, the original label is protected by a trade mark, and any alternative use unauthorised by the original proprietors is punishable by law. In the domain of cultural identity, the punishment is cultural confusion, conflict and, often, war.
- Alternative definitions of cultural identity conflict with, contradict and challenge each other, but all of them agree on the legitimacy of the original definition.
- The insistence on retaining the old name of a culture while giving it a new content – when the original content is still practised – generates an insecure group identity. The innovators – who can never gain legitimacy while the originators are still around – experience this lack of legitimacy as a threat to their identity (that is, the meaning of their existence). They suffer from a psychological insecurity but seek external causes (for example, persecutors) for it. They experience any reference to their origin, jokes about it, or criticism of it, as a threat to their 'existence', and see no difference between cultural and physical existence. They confuse the threat to the meaning of their existence with a threat to their physical existence.

Specific Problems of Jewish Cultural Identity

In addition to the general problems facing those who try to adapt traditional cultural identities to the modern world (all traditional cultures today face similar problems), there are specific problems stemming from the unique features of the Jewish identity.

First of these is the bond between ethnicity and religion in Jewish culture, which differs significantly from the Islamic or Christian cases. Islam does not confer Arab ethnicity, and Arab ethnicity does not depend on Islam. The same holds for Christianity. In the Jewish case, practice of the mitzvot confers ethnicity. Any person who practises the mitzvot becomes a member of the Jewish people. Remaining a Jew without practising the mitzvot is always problematic.

Jewish ethnicity is based – historically and culturally – on religion. The Jewish culture is a religious culture. Religion rather than language, territory, biological origin, economic activity or shared historical experience, binds Jews into an ethnic group. There are ample examples to demonstrate this assertion.

This religio-ethnic bond is publicly celebrated during the Passover feast commemorating God 'passing over' the homes of the Jews in ancient Egypt 3,000 years ago when he smote all the first-born

Egyptian males, thus forcing the Pharaoh to 'let my people go'. It is irrelevant whether this is pure mythology, what matters is the acceptance of this ceremony today as an integral component of 'Jewish identity'. The ceremonial Passover meal – the Seder – is the celebration of the birth of the Jewish nation. It is a religio-ethnic celebration of the religious origin of the Jewish people, the 'birthday party' of Jewish ethnicity

The traditional text (Hagadah) which accompanies this ceremonial meal and is read aloud with every dish, declares the religio-ethnic symbolism of every dish and toast. Anyone who wishes to understand the true nature of Jewish ethnicity should study the Hagadah carefully. Jewish adaptationists and atheists have never produced a viable alternative to the Seder yet insist on celebrating it.

Some try to give it a secular, purely historical, interpretation, thus transforming it into an antiquated religious appendage of an outdated tradition. They read aloud the religious text without accepting what it says. They go through the motions of this ritual not because it is meaningful, but because it is an important component of 'Jewish identity'. Although there have been attempts to secularise the Seder, secular versions have never replaced the religious ceremony for most non-religious Jews. Every year the vast majority of Jews who no longer believe in God celebrate the liberation of the Jewish people from Egypt by God.

Most of the 80 per cent of Jews who do not practise the mitzvot insist on doing a bar mitzvah to their sons. Do they practice the mitzvot? No. But they perform the bar mitzva where they promise to perform mitzvot. This indicates that those who insist on defining themselves as Jews have to participate in religious ceremonies even though they don't believe in God. They never ponder the implications of the title itself. They rarely ask themselves what is the connection between mitzvot and Jewishness. It never occurs to them that in this ceremony they accept the obligation to practise the mitzvot. During the bar mitzvah the new initiate has to read publicly, in the synagogue, the daily chapter from the Bible, and accepts the obligation to practise the mitzvot. In the weeks preceding, the initiate is instructed how to perform the mitzvot. Parents who do not practise the mitzvot, or do not believe in God, but insist all the same that their son have a bar mitzvah, knowing very well that he will never practise the mitzvot either, are sowing the seeds of confusion about Jewish identity.

When atheists insist on performing a religious ceremony celebrating God they reveal – and reinforce – the inadequacy of their atheism and the vulnerability of their secularity. Secular Jews have never produced a total philosophical, historical and psychological critique of Jewish religion. They remain dependent on religion to sustain their secular Jewish identity.

This is demonstrated once again in the Jewish male circumcision ceremony, known as 'brit milah' (covenant of the circumcision), which symbolises the covenant between Abraham (the mythological 'Father of the Nation') and God. The actual circumcision, performed by a religious functionary (mohel), marks the newborn male (at the age of eight days) as a member of the Jewish people. Even those who do not believe in God and his covenant (which marks the Jews as 'God's chosen people') nevertheless insist on doing the brit milah.

In general, despite rejecting religion, most 'Jews' cling to the religious ceremonies like brit milah, bar mitzvah and the Seder. This creates ambivalence and confusion, which increases from one generation to the next, and renders the meaning of Jewish identity ever more muddled. Clinging to ceremonies like brit milah, bar mitzvah and the Seder, with their explicit religious meanings, displays an inability to provide a secular definition of Jewish identity. Those who insist on labelling themselves 'Jews' must perform religious ceremonies even if they no longer believe in the existence of God.

For non-believers these ceremonies present an insoluble dilemma: if they fail to perform them, their Jewish identity becomes very vague; if they do perform them without accepting their original meaning, their identity lacks authenticity. The only way out for those who ceased to believe in God was to try to inject a new meaning into these rituals. This was done by shifting the emphasis from the religious to the ethnic component. Those who have ceased to believe in God but insist that they are still Jews argue that Jews are an ethnic entity and that the original religion is an expendable appendage.

This brings us to a dilemma which originates in the theo-centrism of Jewish religion. In Christianity, which is anthropocentric and which puts loyalty to humanity above all else (symbolised by God sacrificing his son to save humanity), religion and God are a means to an end, the welfare of humanity. Not so Judaism. Judaism is theo-centric and puts loyalty to God above all else (symbolised by the readiness of Abraham to sacrifice his son to God). In Judaism God, and worship of God, are an end unto themselves whereas humanity is a means to an end (to demonstrate the glory of the Creator). Any attempt to subordinate God to humanity or to human needs is blasphemy in Judaism because it makes humanity into an end and God into a means to this end. Therefore the adaptation of Jewish religious ceremonies to the needs of secular Jews is blasphemy, and they will always be at a disadvantage in a cultural confrontation with Jews whose supreme loyalty is to God.

Zionism

The group whose loyalty is to the Jewish state and who consider Jews as an ethnic group and the Jewish religion as an expendable, outdated appendage are the secular Zionists. For many Zionists, the Jewish state is the end, whereas Jewish people are the means. The Zionists believe they can replace – culturally and psychologically – the Jewish God by a secular Jewish state.

However, the fact that 'Zion' is the religious name for Palestine, and that the Zionist flag is based on the Jewish prayer-shawl, reveals once again that the secular Zionists cannot sever the link between Jewish ethnicity and Jewish religion. Secular Jewish nationalism is culturally dependent on the Jewish religion.

Modern technology penetrates geographical and cultural barriers. Like every technology, it is a physical embodiment of a conceptual system based on particular assumptions about the nature of the universe, humanity and their connection. Modern technology is not culturally neutral. It is a product of Objectivist Rationalism.

When traditional societies acquire modern technology they import a cultural 'Trojan horse'; their cultures are invaded, insidiously, by an alien culture. This invasion causes a fragmentation of traditional cultures. They split into three fragments, according to their attitudes to the invasion of the alien culture: isolationists, adaptationists and assimilationists. Each of these three has further sub-divisions, but this does not concern us in this essay.

Isolationists try to isolate themselves culturally (sometimes technologically) from the modern world. In the Jewish case, the Orthodox Jews who strictly obey the mitzvot are isolationists.

Adaptationists try to adapt the original culture to the modern world. The Jewish Reform, Conservative and Reconstructionist congregations are the Jewish adaptationists.

Assimilationists try to 'become like all other people' on a personal – or group – basis. They accept the assumptions of objective rationalism. The Zionists are one group of Jewish assimilationists.

Political Zionism, whose aim was to create a secular Jewish nation-state, was founded by Theodor Herzl in Basle in 1897. The founders of Zionism, such as Herzl, Nordau, Pinsker and Zangwill, were advocates of assimilation. Many of the founding fathers of Zionism started as advocates of personal assimilation. They aspired to become 'a person like all other persons'. Herzl himself thought that 'Jewish identity' was perpetuated primarily by anti-Jewish discrimination and persecution. He expressed his feelings by stating:

> We might perhaps be able to dissolve ourselves without a trace in the surrounding races if we were left in peace for only two generations on end. But we shall not be left in peace ... It is

only pressure that forces us back to the parent stem, only the hatred encompassing us that turns us into strangers once more.[2]

Herzl's belief that in the absence of anti-Jewish discrimination 'Jewish identity' becomes so vague that it would disappear within two generations is a feature of Zionism to this day. Zionism depends on anti-Jewishness to prop its vague, secular, notion of Jewish cultural identity. It is saying: 'I may not have a clear definition of "Jewish identity" but this hardly matters because those who persecute me determine my Jewishness.' This assumption is an insult to the original definition of Jewishness. If you practise the mitzvot you know very well what you are. To give credit to your persecutor for defining you is to add insult to injury.

Having encountered anti-Jewish discrimination Herzl (and Pinsker, Nordau, et al.) shifted his assimilationist efforts from the personal to the collective domain. He began to advocate assimilation of the entire Jewish people. His new goal was to make the Jews 'a nation like all other nations'.

The founding father of political Zionism, Herzl, first proposed collective conversion to Christianity. Later, he changed his proposal to collective conversion to secular nationalism. In 1895, he wrote in his diary:

> About two years ago I wanted to solve the Jewish question, at least in Austria, with the help of the Catholic church. I wished to arrange for an audience with the Pope (not without first assuring myself of the support of the Austrian clerical powers) and say to him: Help us against the anti-Semites and I will lead a great movement for the free and honourable conversion of Jews to Christianity. 'Free and honourable' inasmuch as the leaders of this movement – myself in particular – would remain Jews, and as Jews would urge a conversion to the majority-faith. In broad daylight, at twelve o'clock on a Sunday, the exchange of faith would take place in St. Stephen's Cathedral, with a solemn parade and the peal of bells. Not with shame, as solitary individuals have hitherto gone over, but with a proud gesture. And because the Jewish leaders would remain behind, conducting the people only to the threshold of the church and themselves staying outside, it would elevate the whole performance into a display of utter sincerity.
>
> We, the steadfast leaders, would have constituted the final generation. We would have remained with the faith of our fathers. But we would have made Christians of our children before they reached the age of individual decision after which conversion looks like an act of cowardice or calculation.
>
> As is my custom, I had thought the plan out to the finest detail.[3]

Remaining 'with the faith of the fathers' without sharing the faith is the classic Zionist situation. It is inherently contradictory. A year later, in 1896, Herzl stated his new conviction:

> The idea which I have developed in this situation is an ancient one: it is the establishment of the Jewish state ... I think the Jewish question is neither a social nor a religious one, although it may likewise take these and other forms. It is a national question, which can only be solved by the civilised nations of the world in council. We are a people, one people.[4]

What would make the secular 'Jewish' state specifically Jewish? To this question neither Herzl nor the Zionist movement ever gave a positive answer. Herzl was very explicit that it could not be religion:

> Then shall we have a theocracy? No indeed. Faith unites us, knowledge gives us freedom. We shall therefore not permit any theocratic tendency to emerge among our spiritual authorities. We shall keep them to their synagogues, just as we shall keep our professional army within the confines of our barracks. Army and Rabbinate will be honoured as highly as their valuable functions require and deserve. But they must not interfere in the administration of the State which confers distinction on them or they will conjure up difficulties outside and inside.[5]

Difficulties indeed. In March 1990 Israel was in an uproar after a 20 minute speech by the 96-year-old Rabbi Shach, who advised his followers not to join a coalition government under the leadership of the Ma'arach (Israeli Labour Party) because members of the party violate the mitzvot. Rabbi Shach stated:

> ... the Jew cannot be destroyed. He can be killed but his sons will continue to adhere to the Bible. As long as the Jew does not sever his links with the heritage of his ancestors, he is linked to the scholars, to the righteous, to Abraham, Isaac and Jacob, they were alive. The entire world may be destroyed but the Jew lives forever as long as he clings to the ways of his ancestors and does not seek alien ways and ideology.
> ... A nation that lacks contact with its ancestors is doomed from the start. It will never come to be.
> ... There are kibbutzim which do not know what the Day of Atonement, the Sabbath and the Mikveh [ritual bath] are, they have no idea whatsoever. They raise rabbits and pigs [forbidden to Jews]. Do they have any links to their ancestors? How can this generation survive [as Jews] if they see the father eating on the Day of Atonement?

... One must cut oneself off from the parties which lack any connection to Judaism, some more, some less. Generally they are all the same. They have disengaged themselves from their ancestors. Those who lack a past, what status do they have?[6]

This was the voice of the original Jewish identity denouncing the new versions for betrayal of their origin. The majority of Israelis of Jewish background were outraged by this denunciation, but could neither challenge the Rabbi's definition of Jewishness nor produce a generally accepted alternative. They gave vent to their frustration by extremely abusive rhetoric. Israeli writer Amnon Dankner wrote a reply in the Israeli daily *Hadashot*:

We heard you, senile one. You may return to your historical sewer from which you crawled to utter your idiotic feeble bleat. You, a spiritual leader?

All your banal blabber contained nothing – no depth, no wisdom or enlightenment, no formulation or brilliance, no stimulus to thought. Nothing of your blabber in the sports stadium differed from what an ignorant Jew would pour out in the market-place.

You a scholar of the Bible?

Woe to the Bible that has such scholars.

Listen, for years you have presided here as an arch-louse, first and foremost of the gang of parasites which increases and fattens on our back, sucks our sap and blood, and refuses to join our circulation of blood and pain. You had a great time lately, but don't let this rise to your calcified head. You know very well, feeble of limb and knee, that your power will not last for ever. The day will come when we shall settle scores with you and all other parasites. What you said the day before yesterday only whetted the appetite and brought that date nearer. You increased hatred in Israel. The wages of hatred are – hatred.

You dare to open your toothless mouth against the Kibbutzim? You dare to abuse them? They, whose cemeteries are filled with gravestones of wonderful youths killed while defending the entire nation, including thousands of draft evaders, who serve as your flock. Take off your shoes, dirty old man.

... And you will presumably decide for me who is a Jew and who is not. A new landlord. You will decide that I am not a Jew? Who are you? God?

Have you contracted a dose of megalomania in your old age? Anyone who doesn't wear your laughable garb is not a Jew? Shall we all measure ourselves by your standards? Ma'arakh are not Jewish, Likud are a little Jewish, and the lice are the best? I, for example, do not say that you are not Jewish. You are definitely Jewish. An obscurantist Jew, a primitive, a miserable chatterer, but a Jew.

You do not deserve that we take your analysis seriously, but it is clear that your way leads to regression, degeneration, obscurantism, death and crematoria, whereas our way leads to construction, new life, freedom and light. We will fight you, and maybe you will live to see our victory.

The occupied territories do not matter to you, because no territory matters to you. Tomorrow you would gladly give up Tel-Aviv, because the entire country matters little to you. I don't care whether you go with the Ma'arakh or with the Likud, the main thing is that you go to hell.[7]

This was a typical example of the response of the secular majority in Israel to Rabbi Shach's speech. Dankner is wrong when he thinks that he 'plays fair' with Rabbi Shach by admitting that the Rabbi is a Jew. He simply has no choice. He – and all other secular Jews – can never challenge the validity of the original definition of Jewishness. Rabbi Shach can – and will – always challenge the validity of definitions which differ from the original.

Dankner's weakness is his insistence on defining himself as a Jew. Even the President of Israel, Haim Herzog, could only complain about the Rabbi's assertions when he went to a kibbutz cemetery and declared:

Those who never heard the sound of battle are ready to pin the label of traitor on those who brought the Israel Defence Force in its greatest hour to victories and successes. Anonymous soldiers who risked their lives in the underground for our liberation are suddenly discovering that in the eyes of a handful they are untouchable and repulsive.[8]

Jews who fail to practise the mitzvot reject the original definition of Jewishness, however loyal they are to the Jewish people or to the 'Jewish' state. Israeli patriotism does not confer Jewishness. Many Israeli Arabs of the Druze community volunteered for the Israeli army and died in combat; does this confer Jewishness on them?

Viewed from the original definition of Jewish identity, Rabbi Shach is right and his opponents are wrong. If the State of Israel is not a theocracy – as Herzl and the Zionist movement insisted – its existence is, at best, irrelevant to the efforts to perpetuate the original meaning of Jewishness. The existence of non-believing 'Jews' does not imply the existence of Jewish identity.

Dankner and his like must admit that Rabbi Shach is a Jew; Rabbi Shach has no scruples in denouncing those who fail to practise mitzvot as traitors to Jewishness. Since Shach's loyalty to God (expressed by practising mitzvot) overrides his loyalty to state or nation, he will not hesitate to dissociate himself from them even if they are genuinely Jewish. The Zionists – as long as they insist on defining themselves as Jewish – can never dissociate themselves from brit milah, bar mitzvah, Seder or Rabbi Shach.

Actually, the situation is worse, because the Zionists insist on 'the centrality of Israel in Jewish life' (Jerusalem Programme adopted in 1968 by the 27th World Zionist Congress), that is, that loyalty to their secular state is the core of Jewish identity today. Thus they challenge the primacy of the mitzvot as the definitive feature of 'Jewish identity'. Ever since Korah declared 'all of the congregation are holy, every one of them' (Numbers 26, 3) and in response 'the earth opened her mouth and swallowed them up' (Numbers 26, 32), Jewish ethnocentrism was denounced as blasphemy by Jewish theocentrism.

The Zionists, whose loyalty to their secular state (whose Jewish identity they cannot define without resort to religion) overrides all else, are economically and numerically far stronger than those who practise the mitzvot, but culturally they don't stand a chance against them. The weakness of Israelis who reject the mitzvot is their insistence on calling themselves 'Jews'. If they had the courage to define themselves – culturally – as 'Israelis' rather than as 'Jews', they would rid themselves of their identity complex and of conflicts with people like Rabbi Shach. At present, the majority of secular Israelis insist that their cultural identity is Jewish rather than Israeli.

In 1912, representatives of Jews who practised the mitzvot met in Katowice and formed Agudat Israel ('The Jewish Association') to fight against Zionism. Only a handful (the Mizrahi) joined the Zionists. Most of the religious argued against the Zionists that 'he who leads one to sin is worse than one who kills since killing puts an end to one's existence in this world, but sinning puts an end to it also in the next world'.[9]

If we replace 'next world' by 'this world in the future', and 'sinning' by 'changing the value system', this assertion makes sense. From a cultural point of view, destruction of a culture is worse than destruction of members of the culture. That is why Orthodox Jews like Neturei Karta consider the Zionists as worse than Nazis. The Nazis destroyed Jewish lives but were never a threat to Jewish identity. The Zionists saved some Jewish lives but they are destroying the original Jewish identity.

The use of acrimonious rhetoric against the other side is not the prerogative of secular Zionists like Dankner. One need only read publications by members of Neturei Karta to come across a formulation like:

This is the apogee of the Zionist dream: Normalization. Dance Herzl in your grave. Your dream has come true. Israel is a nation of Barbarians, perverts, of moral and immoral non-entities, like the other nations.

There is nothing Jewish about perversion, smut and zionism. To be a Jew is to loyally and joyfully carry out G-d's commandments; to treasure tradition and to guard it for our children and their future. We will prevail with faith in the Almighty as we await the true redemption.[10]

(The omission of the 'o' in God's title is in the original, conforming to the prohibition of any visual or oral representation of God.)

This quote expresses the gist of the religious argument against secular Zionism: 'normalisation', that is, becoming 'a nation like all other nations' instead of remaining God's nation, is a betrayal of Jewishness. If, moreover, the traitors insist that they are 'central to Jewish life', they become impostors and usurpers.

When Israel was established in 1948, Ben-Gurion, wishing to avoid a cultural confrontation with religious Jewry, offered a compromise: Israeli law on marriage, divorce and burial will be religious law; and religious holidays will be state holidays. Religious Jewry (apart from Neturei Karta) accepted the offer, 'recognised' Israel, and refrained from contesting the 'Jewishness' of this secular state. This arrangement became known as the 'status quo'.

After the conquest of East Jerusalem by secular Zionism in 1967, followers of Rabbi Cook produced a messianic interpretation of Zionism, arguing that it was 'the beginning of [messianic] redemption'. This interpretation produces religious arguments to legitimise annexations by declaring Jerusalem, the West Bank and Gaza to be 'holy'.

However, conferring 'holiness' on any object, be it a land, a wall, or a nation, is a worship of substitutes for God contradicting the theocentric spirit of Judaism. No wonder that Neturei Karta denounce it as blasphemy. The attitude to the Zionist state creates divisions among religious Jews. Is Israel the start of religious redemption, or the new golden calf?

In the last decade political Zionism has started seriously to consider the identity complex of secular Western Jews. The enormous apparatus of Israeli propaganda among Jews throughout the world now promotes the view that identification with Israel resolves the 'Jewish identity' complex. Identification with the 'Jewish' state is projected as the new meaning of Jewishness.

The Zionist slogan of 'the centrality of Israel in Jewish life' is historically false (what did Jews do before Israel existed?), blasphemous (it conflicts with the centrality of God in Jewish life) and shaky (Israel itself cannot agree on the definition of Jewishness). The slogan uses Israel as a veil to hide the impossibility of a secular definition of

Jewish identity and an unbridgeable chasm between secular Zionism and Judaism. 'Secular' and 'Jewish' are contradictory concepts, and hostile cultures. The failure to reconcile the two is deeper in Israel than elsewhere.

The Israeli writer Haim Hazaz summed up the relation between secular Zionism and Judaism in his famous short story 'The Sermon', in which the protagonist Yudka says: 'Zionism and Judaism are not at all the same thing ... Zionism begins with the wreckage of Judaism.'[11]

The Israeli (Ethnic) Identity

The Zionist movement set out to create a secular Jewish state. It succeeded in establishing Israel in 1948. This state was to serve both as a refuge for Jews fleeing from persecution and as a source for a new, secular, Jewish ethnic identity. Two, even three, generations of 'Jews' have been born and have grown up in Israel. Despite the fact that this is, from an anthropological point of view, a short span of time, it has sufficed to create a new cultural identity which has little in common with the original Jewish identity – the new secular Israeli ethnicity.

Israeli ethnic identity is shared by people brought up in Hebrew in a secular Israeli culture, that is, rejecting religion and mitzvot. It differs qualitatively from Jewish cultural identity. It is unique and recognisable.

A good description of such attitudes is given by the Israeli writer Amos Oz quoting a monologue by one such Israeli:

> As far as I am concerned, you can call me whatever you like. Call me a monster, call me a murderer, but kindly indicate that I do not hate Arabs. On the contrary. Personally I feel much better among them – particularly the Beduins, than I do among the Zhids. [Russian abusive term for Jews]
>
> The Arabs, those that we haven't spoiled yet, are proud people, rational, but cruel or generous according to circumstances. The Zhids are completely twisted. If you want to try to straighten them out, you have to bend them really hard in the other direction. And that, in a nutshell, is my whole thesis. As far as I'm concerned, you can call the State of Israel by any pejorative you like. Call it Judeo-Nazi, the way Professor Leibowitz did. Why not? How does the saying go – 'better a live Judeo-Nazi than a dead saint'? Me, I don't mind being Qaddafi. I'm not looking to the gentiles for admiration and I don't need their love. But I don't need it from your kind of Jew either. I want to survive. And my intention happens to be that my

children will survive too. With or without the blessings of the
Pope and assorted Torah sages from the New York Times.[12]

Such views are not upheld by all Israelis, but the need to justify
the state of Israel, a personal self-image welded to the public image
of Israel, is shared by most Israelis.

According to Baruch Kurzweil, a founder of the religious Bar-
Ilan University in Israel, the Israeli is 'a Hebrew-speaking gentile'.[13]

The 'Hebrew-speaking gentile' has a secure (secular) cultural
identity, and no 'identity complex' (nobody doubts his Israeliness),
unless he insists on defining himself as 'Jewish' rather than as
'Israeli'. Secular Israelis who define themselves as 'Jews' immediately plunge into the difficulties confronting anyone who wants to
define a secular 'Jewish identity'.

Amos Oz quotes the reply of Israel Harel, a leader of the religious
settlers on the West Bank, to the question 'Where is the major
barricade in Israel right now?' (autumn 1981):

> The major barricade is the one that divides the Jews from the
> Israelis. The Jews are those who want to live, to one degree or
> another, in accordance with the Bible. The Israelis pay
> lip service, maybe, to the heritage, but in essence they aspire
> to be a completely new people here, a satellite of Western
> culture.
> ... The battle between the 'Jews' and the 'Israelis' is being
> determined much too early for my taste, and in the wrong bat-
> tlefield, in the political-military-emotional arena, and not, as I
> would prefer, in the arena of spiritual confrontation.
> ... with the covert and overt atheism, with the 'relevancy',
> with all the fashionable 'Israeli-ism' influenced by America, with
> the 'normalisation' of Ammon Rubinstein and A.B.
> Yehoshua,they really don't have any connection [to Jewishness]
> any more.[14]

The Zionists are horrified that their departure from the original
(religious) Jewish identity, their efforts to normalise the Jews and
make them 'a nation like all the other nations', has produced a non-
Jew. They try – in vain – to deny this reality. The fact is that living
daily – secular – life in Israel as a member of the cultural majority,
speaking Hebrew at home and outside, produces a group identity
very different from that of Jews who live outside Israel, constantly
experience themselves as a cultural minority, don't speak Hebrew
at home but only during traditional ceremonies. The cleavage
between the two experiences inevitably produces a cleavage of
group identities.

The Effects of the Fragmentation of Group Identity

The Survival Complex

The fact that there are now two, three or more Jewish identities produces uncertainty about the meaning of the term. Many feel threatened by this uncertainty. They develop an anxiety about the meaning of their identity. They become obsessed with the survival of their identity. 'Survival' becomes their mode of existence. They don't 'live', they 'survive'. They are constantly preoccupied with their 'struggle for survival', and see threats to this survival everywhere. They lose the distinction between physical existence and cultural existence. Their existence is shaped by their anxiety.

The psychoanalyst R.D. Laing described an argument between two of his patients:

> An argument occurred between two patients in the course of a session in an analytic group. Suddenly one of the protagonists broke off the argument to say: 'I can't go on. You are arguing in order to have the pleasure of triumphing over me. At best you win an argument, at worst you lose an argument. I am arguing in order to preserve my existence.'[15]

Although this patient is defending his argument, not his body, he no longer distinguishes between the two. This patient is suffering from an anxiety about his 'existence'. It no longer matters to him whether he is threatened by an argument or by a gun. All he knows is that he must defend his 'existence'.

Laing adds:

> This patient was a young man who I would say was sane, but, as he stated, his activity in the argument, as in the rest of his life, was not designed to gain gratification, but to defend 'his existence' ... A firm sense of one's own autonomous identity is required in order that one may be related as one human being to another. Otherwise, any and every relationship threatens the individual with loss of identity.[16]

A similar state of mind permeates the UJS (UK Union of Jewish Students) pamphlet which accuses anti-Zionists of being Jew-haters. Consider the following assertion in the pamphlet: '... there is the fourth form of antisemitism destroying the Jews by promoting assimilation. This form of antisemitism is prevalent among much of the ultra-left and it dominates RETURN. If the programme laid out by Bourne, Machover and others [in RETURN] is fulfilled, then Hitler will gain a posthumous victory – the Jews will be destroyed.'[17]

The person who wrote these words, and those on the UJS council who endorsed them, can no longer distinguish between Hitler's physical extermination of Jews, and assimilation. A mixed marriage (between Jew and non-Jew), which is one form of assimilation, becomes Hitler's victory. The fact that in a mixed marriage the person is alive (perhaps even happy), whereas in Hitler's victory Jews are physically exterminated, no longer matters to the author of the UJS pamphlet. A mixed marriage is equated with a gas chamber. If this logic, which no longer distinguishes between the physical and mental, is accepted, we erase the distinction between the physical and the mental.

After quoting what they describe as Moshe Machover's view in RETURN that 'there is no material basis for the existence of Jewish communities outside Israel' (a thesis one can discuss rationally), the pamphlet pours out the following invective: 'This is not progressive Marxist analysis, it is cultural genocide, seeking the destruction of the Jews, culturally, politically, religiously, and socially.'[18]

'Seeking the destruction of the Jews' ascribes active, malicious, intentions. Using the term 'genocide', which means physical extermination of a racial group, in an argument about assimilation reveals again the lack of distinction between the physical and the mental. Nowhere in Machover's article is there anything suggesting, however remotely, a policy of destruction. The fact that the anonymous UJS author uses again and again terms like 'destruction of the Jews', 'genocide', 'Jew-haters', gives us an idea about the kind of anxieties that torment him/her. The author's sense of existence as a Jew is rather precarious, hence he/she is constantly struggling for 'survival'.

Divergence of Codes – End of Communication

The theme which runs like a thread throughout the pamphlet is the assertion that anyone who criticises Zionism (that is, secular Jewish nationalism) is criticising all Jews and is therefore an anti-Jewish racist. It describes the writers in RETURN as: 'a group of Jews, coalescing around the magazine called RETURN, who peddle antisemitism under the guise of anti-Zionism.'[19]

As writers in RETURN state explicitly that being a Zionist (that is, upholding specific political views) and being a Jew (that is, sharing a cultural identity) are two different things, the UJS author decides that this is merely a ploy. 'Zionists' is just a code for 'Jews', asserts the pamphlet. It states: 'RETURN use the tragedies of modern history, particularly the Holocaust, as well as antisemitic theory, to attack present day Zionists (a code for "Jews")'. RETURN is 'using "Zionists" as a code word'.[20]

The assertion that for RETURN 'Zionists' is just 'a code' for 'Jews' is the cornerstone of the entire UJS pamphlet. But the moment one states 'I hereby announce that "A" is a code for "B" ', we are in the domain of private codes. There is no possibility of meaningful discussion with someone who constructs a private code. Communication of meanings becomes impossible when the codes for the symbols differ. The only useful approach is to analyse the nature of the private code. The moment the UJS pamphlet ceases to relate to the word that is actually printed on paper, namely 'Zionists', and begins to interpret it as 'a code for "Jews" ', it crosses the boundary from common meaning to private meaning.

Complex of Persecution

Orthodox Jews vehemently reject equating 'Jews' with Zionists; are they 'antisemitic' too? If we are to follow the logic of the UJS pamphlet that 'Zionism' is a code for 'Jews' and 'anti-Zionism is antisemitic racism', then anti-Zionist Orthodox Jews are also guilty of 'antisemitic malice' and are 'antisemitic racists'. The absurdity of this conclusion reveals the argument as a persecutory delusion.

Since Orthodox Jews reject the equating of Zionism with Jews – and they have far more authority than UJS to decide this issue – we have to consider the possibility that the UJS writer has constructed a private view of the world wherein this equating is valid. As this private view equates criticism (of Zionism) with (anti-Jewish) racism, we have to conclude that the writer suffers persecutory delusions. The delusion is experienced as reality.

It is customary to explain this persecutory delusion as a side-effect of the Holocaust. However, the fact that Orthodox Jews who suffered in the Holocaust do not suffer persecutory delusions, while some members of the UJS council – born 25 years after the Holocaust – do, forces us to look for other causes. In most cases, the cause is an insecure sense of Jewish identity.

RETURN, like other anti-Zionist Jewish groups (for example, the religious Neturei Karta group), criticises Zionism for accepting the idea that Jews must leave Europe (and emigrate to Palestine), an idea promoted later by the Nazis. RETURN also criticises Zionism for putting loyalty to the Zionist state above loyalty to the Jewish people, for its reluctance to save Jews from Nazi Europe unless they went to Palestine – a fact admitted by Zionist sources.[21] An anti-Zionist argument indeed, but in what way is it anti-Jewish?

The UJS pamphlet declares that the authors of RETURN 'pose a serious threat to the identity, well-being and outlook of the Jewish community' (p. 2). How can a magazine pose a threat (serious or not) to an identity, or to an outlook?

The pamphlet purports to reveal 'the essential similarities between the antisemitism of the National Front and that of RETURN' (p. 2). It quotes John O'Mahoney: 'the whole left "anti-Zionist" campaign against the Jews – yes, against the Jews – is part of a cultural ferment that can lead to a full-fledged persecution of the Jews' (p. 30). It states: '*RETURN*'s "anti-Zionist" campaign is a cover for their campaign against the Jewish people' (p. 30); and 'their sole raison d'etre is to attack, vilify and de-legitimise Jews and Judaism' (p. 2).

As no article in *RETURN* made any criticism of Jews we have to conclude that the author of the UJS pamphlet – whom we assume to be honest – suffers from an anxiety which makes him/her interpret criticism of Zionism as a veiled, coded, malicious, racist attack on Jews. One cause for this anxiety is a foggy, insecure, Jewish identity; another is an insecure Zionist identity.

Until the Second World War, Zionists (who numbered about 5 per cent of world Jewry) preached emigration to Palestine and creation of a Jewish state there. They practised what they preached. They emigrated to Palestine and did their best to promote a Jewish state there. In 1948 the Zionist state was established, but world Jewry failed to emigrate there. Most Jews who did emigrate to Israel after 1948 were not Zionists. Ben-Gurion used to say after 1948, 'the immigrants are not Zionists, and the Zionists don't immigrate'. A popular joke was 'A Zionist is a Jew who pays another Jew to go to Palestine'.

Since 1948 Zionism has been in a crisis of identity. The state exists, but the greater part of world Jewry does not immigrate. The majority of the Israelis are not Zionists, they consider Zionism an anachronism. The subject of their nationalism is Israeliness, not world Jewry. To be a Zionist and live outside Israel is to preach one thing and practise another. Authentic Zionists practised emigration to Palestine. Most Zionists today live outside Israel and have no intention of emigrating. This creates a flawed Zionist identity. Such people salve their troubled Zionist conscience by frantic fund-raising and lobbying for Israel. Their pro-Israel activity is motivated by an insecure Jewish identity and an insecure Zionist identity. Insecurity is a powerful drive, in political as well as personal life.

Those who practise the mitzvot can teach the UJS author a very useful lesson: you define yourself by what you practice, not by what you declare yourself to be. This does not nullify the significance of one's declarations. It transforms them from statements of fact into declarations of a wish. These people are, in their actual way of life, no different from non-Jews around them, but they wish to be known, to themselves and to others, as 'Jews', while unclear what that means. The conflict between fact and wish can yield insights, but factual self-definition is determined by one's practice, not by one's wish.

If you practise mitzvot, you are defined by the mitzvot. If you practise anxieties about Jewish survival, identity and existence, you are defined by these anxieties. If you practise struggle against all forms of oppression, you are a humanist. If you fix every morning, you are a junkie. If you studied medicine but work as a writer, you are not a doctor. If you preach political, social and economic equality but practise vanguardism, you are an elitist, not a socialist.

We are what we practise, not what we declare ourselves to be.

Notes and References

1. First published in *RETURN*, June 1990.
2. Theodor Herzl, *The Jewish State*, 1956, Tel-Aviv: Newman, p. 60.
3. *The Diaries of Theodor Herzl* (ed. Marvin Lowenthal 1958), London: Gollancz, p. 7
4. *The Jewish State*, pp. 29, 38.
5. *The Jewish State*, p. 135.
6. *Ha'Aretz*, 28 March 1990, p. 2.
7. *Hadashot*, 28 March 1990, p. 5.
8. *Hadashot*, 30 March 1990.
9. Rashi, *Midrash Rabah*, Chapter 23, p. 9.
10. Neturei Karta magazine, the *Jewish Guardian*, summer 5746, 1986, p. 7.
11. Haim Hazaz, 'The Sermon', in R. Alter (ed.), *Modern Hebrew Literature*, 1975, New York: Behrman House, p. 273.
12. Amos Oz, *In the Land of Israel*, 1983, Fontana, p. 87.
13. Baruch Kurzweil, *Facing the Spiritual Perplexity of Our Times*, 1976, Bar-Ilan University Press, p. 224.
14. Oz, *In the Land of Israel*, pp. III5–6.
15. R.D. Laing, 1964, *The Divided Self*, Pelican, p. 43.
16. Laing, *The Divided Self*, pp. 43, 44.
17. Anon, *RETURN: Jews and Jew-Haters*, 1990, UJS, p. 5.
18. *RETURN: Jews and Jew-Haters*, pp. 4–5.
19. *RETURN: Jews and Jew-Haters*, p. 2.
20. *RETURN: Jews and Jew-Haters*, pp. 33, 16.
21. See Shabtai Bet-Hatzvi, *Post-Ugandan Zionism in the Crisis of the Holocaust* (Hebrew), 1977, Tel-Aviv: Bronfman.

3

Generations and Cultures in Israel[1]

Unlike many other countries in the world, the state of Israel, and Israeli society, are the creations of a deliberate and organised effort of a movement known as political Zionism.[2] This does not mean that the Israelis themselves are conscious Zionists. Most of them are not. It does mean, however, that the political, civil and social institutions in Israel are conscious constructs of political Zionism, and embody its assumptions. The Israelis themselves, their mentality, assumptions, aspirations, motivations and attitudes are constantly shaped by these institutions. Most Israelis are unaware of this conditioning and tend to take their resulting attitudes as 'natural'. The following essay points out some of the components which go into the making of the dominant personality structure in Israel.

Political Zionism did not fall out of the blue, it had its cultural antecedents in Jewish history,[3] its social milieu among the Jews persecuted in Tsarist Russia, and its political leaders from the assimilationist milieu in Western Europe. Yet until the Second World War only a minority of world Jewry supported political Zionism, and that movement could never pretend to appear as representative of all Jews. Political Zionism had to defend itself against religious Jewry, assimilationist Jewry and cultural Zionists.

Religious Jews argue that revival of Jewish political independence is God's task and should not be interfered with by human action. Moreover, they remembered the cultural fiasco caused by a similar attempt in the seventeenth century.

The assimilationists argued that a Jewish state would necessarily be based on a discrimination between Jew and non-Jew which was precisely what they were opposed to in the countries in which they lived. How could they support such discrimination in the Jewish state while struggling against it in the country of their abode?

The cultural Zionists argued that a political revival (that is, establishing a Jewish state) would be meaningless without a cultural revival. They emphasised that it was not only the Jews who emerged from the ghettoes but the Jewish culture[4] as well. They pointed out that outside the ghetto Jews encountered modern, secular cultures and started to give up – in growing numbers – their traditional religious culture. If Jewishness was to depend on a faith in which most Jews no longer believed, then Jewish identity was bound to become meaningless for the non-religious majority. Even those who adhered to the religion encountered considerable problems due to the fact that there was no reformation in Judaism parallel to Protestantism in Christianity. The Jewish faith is a fossil.[5]

The cultural Zionists, in particular A'had-Ha'am, recognised the significance of this problem and argued for a modernisation of the Jewish culture which would retain many of its traditions yet liberate it from the grip of religion. He proposed the creation of a cultural, rather than political, centre in Palestine, to revive the Hebrew language, literature, poetry, etc.

The political Zionists rejected this view. Their leaders, like Herzl and Nordau, came from an assimilationist background and had little or no awareness of the Jewish culture. It was only when their attempts at assimilation were frustrated by the anti-semitic prejudices of the European bourgeoisie (for example, the Dreyfus trial) that the idea of a Jewish nation-state occurred to them. From its beginning to this day political Zionism depends constantly on two external elements: anti-semitism and failed assimilation. The political Zionists elevated their frustrated assimilation to the rank of a historical truth, namely, that anti-semitism is a permanent feature of mankind and cannot be overcome. They argued that the enigma of secular 'Jewish identity' was irrelevant because it was the anti-semites who defined a Jew. They insisted on the creation of 'the state of the Jews' (that is, a refuge to those fleeing from persecution) rather than the creation of a 'Jewish state' (that is, a state permeated by a uniquely Jewish culture).

To this the cultural Zionists replied that unless Jewish culture itself was updated there was no point in diverting all the energy of the Jewish people towards the creation of a state that would be just another state; victims of anti-semitism seeking refuge could go to any country willing to accept them rather than to a state of the Jews which would have nothing meaningfully 'Jewish' about it.

The questions around which the debate centred were:

Was the Jewish culture doomed to a fossilised existence in its religious form?
What is the meaning of secular Jewishness in the absence of anti-semitism?
What would secular Jewishness mean in a secular Jewish state?
Can statehood provide a solution to the problem of cultural identity?

Eighty years have elapsed since the controversy over these issues raged between the political and the cultural Zionists. Moreover, 'the state of the Jews' has now been in existence for almost a quarter of a century. Under these circumstances one can reformulate the old questions thus:

Has Israel provided a solution to the problem of (secular) Jewish identity?
What is the new, secular Jewish identity, which the creation of Israel has brought about?

In discussing these issues we shall follow the history of the dominant culture in Israel, namely that of the European secular Jews. We shall not refer to the culture of the Palestinian Arabs or that of the oriental Jews despite their richness and uniqueness, since they are subordinate cultures in Israel. They did not create Israel, nor do they sustain it culturewise, but are themselves living under the constant pressure of the dominant Euro-secular culture.

The European Jews in Israel constitute three generations each with a different experience and mentality. The three generations whose attitudes we outline here are:

1. the founding fathers, 1880–1918
2. the settlers, 1918–1948
3. the third-generation, 1948–

The Founding Fathers (1880–1918)

Secular European Jewry is the social group whose culture dominates Israel. These are the people who founded political Zionism and formed its backbone and muscle in every sense. They struggled for the creation of Israel and, having achieved this, they moulded its politics, institutions, economics, army and society. They hold all key positions and take all crucial decisions. They determine in detail the education of the young. It is for these reasons that this group – rather than the religious minority in Israel – is responsible for the outcome.

Religious Jewry was never keen on political Zionism, nor did it play any significant role in that movement. Religious Jews would go to Palestine to be buried but not to establish a Jewish state. The Orthodox leadership never forgot the cultural catastrophe brought about by the Shabtai Tsvi movement in the seventeenth century, when a similar political attempt failed. From their point of view the 'redemption of Israel' is God's task, and human interference with divine roles was bound to end in disaster. Even today many religious Jews in Israel and elsewhere have an ambiguous (sometimes even hostile) attitude to the Zionist state.

Zionism, whether political or cultural, is in a different position, for it depends on the Jewish religion. Why establish a state in Palestine (that is, Zion) rather than in Africa? Why invoke the Old Testament as a justification for such a choice? Why all this insistence on the 'divine rights' or 'historical rights' of all Jews over the whole of Palestine?

From the day that the first Zionist Congress declared its aim – 'To create for the Jewish people a home in Palestine' – (1897), until the day a 'Jewish State' was declared in Palestine (1948), it was the aspiration, effort and activity to found that state which endowed the life of Zionist individuals and groups with a meaning and thus with a culture. Every act of Zionist Jews and non-Jews, in Palestine or elsewhere, acquired a significance, and a positive – or negative – value according to its contribution, or hindrance of, the efforts to create that state.[6] Under those circumstances it seemed as though the question of secular Jewishness and its meaning was a scholastic debate.

Only after achieving statehood did this issue surface again: what is the meaning of Jewishness in a secular Jewish state? This time, however, the debate raged not among intellectuals but among lawyers. The issue itself took on a legal robe because the Israeli legal system, legislated by secular Zionists, contains the term 'Jew' as a legal concept. Not only is marital law subordinated to direct religious ruling[7] but automatic right of immigration and citizenship is granted only to one whom the law defines as 'Jew'. That, after all, was the main purpose of the Zionist endeavour. No one foresaw the problems that would emerge from embedding the term 'Jew' in the legal system.

The issue exploded for the first time in the mid 1950s with the case of Fr Daniel Rufeisen who was brought up as a Jew in Poland but converted to Catholicism. Rufeisen arrived in Israel as a Catholic monk to join a monastery. He asked for automatic rights of immigration and citizenship, defining himself as a Jew due to his ethnic origin and as a catholic due to his religion. The Ministry of the Interior (the traditional stronghold of the religious political parties) rejected his request and he appealed to the High Court because, according to Jewish religious law, being born to a Jewish mother made him a Jew even though he converted to Catholicism.

The secular court was asked to decide whether Rufeisen was a 'Jew' from a legal point of view, but the authority of the court was immediately challenged by the religious authorities. This raised a whole new set of questions: who is qualified to decide who is a Jew? by what authority? according to what criteria? Rufeisen himself? the court? a government committee? the religious authorities?

A passionate debate over these issues divided Israelis. People felt their identity to be threatened. The secular majority argued that their Jewish ethnicity did not depend on acceptance of the Jewish religion, and that Rufeisen's request should be granted. The judges argued that subjective feelings of being 'Jewish ethnically' were an insufficient basis for a ruling and that no definition of Jewishness was possible unless one took religion into account (a non-believer is considered a Jew if his mother was a Jew). The judges agreed that according to religious law Rufeisen was still a Jew, despite converting to Catholicism, but that according to secular law his conversion disqualified him.[8]

The case was over, but the issue was not. It erupted repeatedly. A recent case (in January 1970) was that of an Israeli naval officer, Major Shalit, married to an atheist Scottish girl, who requested that their children be registered as 'ethnically Israelis, or Hebrews' (Israeli law and identity cards require every citizen to be registered by ethnic origin). The Ministry of the Interior rejected the request. The man appealed to the Supreme Court, which deliberated the complexity and history of the issue for weeks and finally ruled by a majority of one to grant the request. The religious political parties immediately threatened to leave the coalition government unless the law be modified so as to prevent the court ruling from becoming a legal precedent. The law was modified according to their demand.

When the issue was debated in Parliament, Mrs Meir, the Prime Minister, made a highly emotional statement, saying:

> On this occasion I wish to state my credo from this rostrum ... more than anything else in this world I value one thing: the existence of the Jewish People. This is more important to me than the existence of the State of Israel, or of Zionism; for without the existence of the Jewish people the others are neither necessary nor can they exist.
>
> ... It is true that nowadays there is no threat of extermination, no threat to the physical existence of the Jewish People ... but there is another threat, a great threat ... namely, mixed marriages in numbers that scare me. Some say it is only 18 percent, some insist on 20 percent, some say that on the campuses in the U.S.A. the figures reach 25 percent. For me the smallest figure of 18 to 20 percent suffices. Any statistician can calculate with pencil and paper what will happen to us. One calamity already hit us: When an independent, free, Jewish state was established in our fatherland, six million Jews were no more. It is intolerable that just when we have a Jewish state the number of mixed marriages goes up – meaning that the number of Jews goes down. This haunts me and, I am sure, many of us, continuously ... those who say this is no business of the State of Israel are wrong. This is perhaps our main role after security, and linked to it. It is worth paying any price for the State of Israel and its security provided one recognized that its role is to preserve the Jewish People.
>
> ... I am not a religious person but no one will uproot from my mind the conviction that without our religion we would have been like all other peoples who once existed and later disappeared.

> ... I know these are new times, modern times, and we must progress. True ... but we must see to it that there will be Jews in the twenty-first century too.
>
> ... Someone has suggested to the government, or to the Attorney General, that perhaps the government will delete 'ethnic origin' from the legal system. As this is not a court ruling, I am entitled to criticize it. I reject this proposal ... Do you suggest, on the twenty-second anniversary of the Jewish State, to throw away the prayer shawl and the phylacteries? A small thing – delete the word 'ethnicity'[8] and create – perhaps not a reality but an impression amongst the Jewish People that they are separate from us, and we are Hebrews, Canaanites, Yevusites, I don't know what else, but not Jews. That they are Jews but we are not?[9]

Anyone who knows Mrs Meir's generation[10] knows that hers is the typical rather than the exceptional view. Mrs Meir did not say all this just to appease the religious political parties or to apologise to her own non-religious party members. She stated the belief which motivates all her politics. A majority for the religious parties' motion that the High Court ruling in favour of Major Shalit's request will not become a legal precedent was secured behind the scenes well before the debate.

Moreover, no political bargaining required the Prime Minister to state that there was something more important to her than the existence of the state she headed, nor can coalition haggling account for a statement by this ardent Zionist that there is something more important to her than Zionism. These utterances reveal a deeper drive than coalition politics. 'I am not ... religious ... but without religion we would have disappeared.' 'I know these are modern times ... but we must see to it that there will be Jews in the twenty-first century ...' '...there is no threat of physical extermination ... to the Jewish People ... but there is another threat, a great threat ... namely, mixed marriages ...'. Each of these passages and their 'buts' reveals the failure of political Zionism to sustain secular Jewishness. The 'survival' of the Jewish people is no longer equated with sheer physical existence, as the founders of political Zionism argued against the cultural Zionists, but becomes something that depends on religion. Without religion the Jews would have disappeared, not physically, but culturally. And today, it is mixed marriages that constitute the major threat to Jewish 'existence'. All this would sound plausible if it came from a religious Jew, but Mrs Meir, typical of her generation, remains a staunch non-believer.

Why is 'mixed' marriage considered such a threat? What is mixed with what? Even those who agree with Mrs Meir – and many non-religious Jews in Israel and elsewhere share her conscious views and subconscious fears – must realise that when a culture depends for its existence on court rulings, its existence is very feeble indeed. Religious Jewry needs no such external support. If cultural existence nowadays looms more urgent than physical existence for political Zionists, yet can only be safeguarded by laws against mixed marriages, one must conclude that the problem of a secular Jewish culture is as acute as it ever was, and that the state of Israel aggravates the problem rather than solves it.

Mrs Meir's generation – in Israel and elsewhere – suffers not only from persecution and identity complexes, but also from what could be called a 'survival complex'. To understand this is one thing, to understand what happens when these complexes produce a political system, a state, is a different matter.

Instead of alleviating identity complexes this state creates new ones, not the least of which is a principled insistence on maintaining internal ethnic discrimination. Not only is every Israeli citizen required to register by ethnic origin and to carry an identity card stating ethnic origin, but the declaration of independence which pledges itself to 'uphold full social and political rights of all citizens without distinction of religion, race or sex' deliberately omits the phrase 'or ethnic origin'. Social and demographic statistical surveys in Israel categorise the population into two groups, namely Jews and non-Jews (see any statistical annual abstract of Israel published by the Central Bureau of Statistics), which indicates that ethnic discrimination is not some minor flaw in the structure of Israel but its fundamental feature.

The Settlers (1918–1948)

In the previous section we dealt with those who, like Mrs Meir, left their countries, homes, and often their families, and emigrated to Palestine with the purpose of creating there a Jewish state. It is their children, born or educated in Palestine under British rule, who constitute the second generation. These are people whose experience was shaped by perpetual struggle during the period of 1918–48 against the Palestinians and the British. Mr Dayan is a typical representative of this generation.

Dayan's generation has no persecution or identity complex. They have neither the desire nor the ability to understand such complexes, and consider them 'inferiority complexes of the Diaspora Jew'. They 'understand' the anti-semites for despising diaspora Jews. The underlying attitude of this generation is one of 'creating accomplished facts'. It was the constant application of this principle to all dealings with the Palestinians and British rulers that brought about the creation of Israel. It remains the guiding principle of all Israeli politics. However, it has gradually spilled over from politics into all social relations and permeates the mentality of that generation.

The deep identification of this generation is neither with the 'Jewish people' nor with Zionism but with 'the state'. However, by 'the state' they do not mean the body politic but a value system. Thus, the Israeli equivalent to 'un-American' in the USA is not 'un-Jewish' or 'anti-Zionist', but 'anti-state'.

It is common among this generation to use the term 'Zionism' in a derogatory sense as an equivalent to 'empty sloganising', while at the same time accepting the moral and ideological leadership of their parents' generation. Dayan's generation has never rebelled against Ben-Gurion's. An insight into this mentality is provided by Dayan's speech to graduates of the Staff and Command course in 1968:

> ... as early as 1928 ... it became clear how difficult it is to implement Zionism and still keep in line with the demands of universal ethics ... was there no other way for Zionism than to deteriorate into pointless chauvinism? Is there no way of assigning a growing sphere of activity to a growing number of Jews without dispossessing the Arabs?
>
> ... surely the day is not far off when no more uninhabited land will be available and the settling of a Jew will lead automatically to the dispossession of a Palestinian peasant? ... on every site where we purchase land and settle people, the present cultivators will, inevitably, be dispossessed. It is our destiny to be in a state of continual warfare with the Arabs. This may well be undesirable but such is reality.[11]

This talk was no exercise in electioneering or party politics. Its purpose was to counter moral dilemmas created in the Israeli army by the Palestinian guerrilla war; a war that many of the Israeli second and third generation recognised as a struggle for national liberation. Unlike Ben-Gurion and Mrs Meir's generation, who consider the Arabs as just another brand of anti-semites, Dayan, a typical representative of his generation, recognises the Palestinians as a dispossessed people with a justifiable – if unacceptable – cause.

In this situation the second Zionist generation faces a dilemma: whether to follow a humane moral code, which does not discriminate between human beings, or to live by a morality which does discriminate and puts loyalty to the Jewish state above all else. Opting for the latter, they see this not as their choice but as their pre-ordained 'destiny'.

If one accepts that what people label as their 'destiny' is often material from their subconscious, created in turn by the cultural conditioning of their parents, one gains insights into the propagation of complexes from one generation to the next. The second generation is caught up in a perpetual conflict with the Palestinians, and feels vaguely that this is not exclusively the Palestinians' fault, but blames some 'destiny' which it cannot identify. The cause, however, is nothing other than the acceptance of the principle that Israel must be a 'Jewish' state wherein Arabs can never share equal political rights; a principle which the second generation accepted – without critical thought – from their parents (whose Jewish complexes they look down upon).

The Third Generation (1948–)

The consciousness of the generation born in independent Israel after 1948 is moulded by the state educational system. The educational syllabus, which all schools must teach, is made up by the Ministry of Education – whose authority was in the hands of the founders generation and only recently passed into the hands of the second generation (Alon replaced Aran as Minister of Education in 1968). The teachers themselves come mainly from the second generation. Those with the 'survival complex' devised the educational system; those with the 'accomplished facts' mentality execute it.

The products are to be seen in the third generation. Already in the early 1950s special lessons on 'Jewish consciousness' were introduced into all schools to inculcate Jewish identity into the minds of the very young. These lessons present Jewish history as a unique – and inexplicable – martyrology: 'Every generation [of gentiles] tries anew to exterminate us, but He saves us from their hands.' Later, the Massada episode (where Hebrew warriors besieged by the Romans preferred to commit suicide rather than surrender) was added to the list. The motto is: 'Massada will never fall again.'

What sort of mentality does this education produce? Dr G. Tamarin, an Israeli psychologist, investigated this question in 1963. He published his results in a document entitled: *A Pilot Study in Chauvinism: The Influence of Ethnico-Religious Prejudices on Moral Judgement*. The research presented 1,066 school children of ages 8 to 14 with two texts and asked them to answer two questions concerning each text and to explain their answers. The answers were later analysed.

The main part of the first text reads:

> You are well acquainted with the following passages from the book of Joshua: 'So the people shouted when the priests blew the trumpets; and it came to pass when the people heard the sound of the trumpet and the people shouted with a great shout and the wall fell down flat, so that the people went into the city every man straight ahead and they took the city. And they utterly destroyed all that was in the city, both man and woman, young and old, and ox, and sheep, and ass with the edge of the

sword. (VI, 20, 21) And that day Joshua took Makkedah, and smote it with the edge of the sword and the kings thereof he utterly destroyed and all the souls that were therein; he let none remain in it; but did unto the king thereof as he did unto the king of Jericho.'

The children were then asked to answer the following questions:

1. Do you think that Joshua, and the Sons of Israel acted right or not?
    Explain your view.
2. Suppose the Israeli army conquers an Arab village in battle. Do you think it would be proper to act against the inhabitants as did Joshua with the people of Jericho and Makkedah? Explain your view.

Out of the total of 1,066 children questioned, the number of those who fully approved of Joshua's method and its application to the Arabs was around 600; about 200 expressed total disapproval; the rest expressed partial approval or disapproval.

The same children were then presented with a 'Chinese version' of the same story, which read:

General Lin, who founded the Chinese kingdom some 3,000 years ago went to war with his army to conquer them a land. They came to some great cities with high walls and strong fortresses. The Chinese War God appeared to General Lin in a dream and promised him victory, ordering him to kill all living souls in the cities, because these people belonged to other religions. General Lin and his soldiers took the towns and utterly destroyed all that was therein, both man and woman, young and old, and ox and sheep, and ass with the edge of the sword. After destroying the cities they continued their way conquering many countries.

They were then asked 'Do you think that General Lin and his soldiers acted right or wrong? Explain your view.'

The answers were classified as above. The number of those who totally approved of Lin's method was about 70; those who totally disapproved about 750; the rest expressed partial approval or disapproval.

The analysis of the answers was:

	A	B	C
On the Joshua question:	60%	20%	20%
On the General Lin:	7%	18%	75%

where: A = total approval
        B = partial approval or disapproval
        C = total disapproval

The various schools selected for the sample covered the entire range of social groups, all social classes, all types of settlements (kibbutzim included) – only Arab schools were exempted. The results are unequivocal. Some of the justifications given by the children merit quoting:

> The Israeli army would have acted rightly if it acted towards the Arabs as Joshua acted towards the people of Jericho and Makeddah. I think so because if they would have left the people and the city, the Arabs would have invaded the city again and fought them.
> I think they acted well, as Joshua did, because the Arabs want us to believe in their idols.
> Joshua and the Sons of Israel did not act well, as they could have spared the animals for themselves.
> Joshua acted properly because the people who inhabited the land were of a different religion, when Joshua killed them he wiped their religion from the earth.
> Nowadays it is not done, but I think then it should have been done.
> This behaviour was necessary, the Arabs are our enemies from always and the Jews did not have a country, and it was necessary to behave like this towards the Arabs.
> Joshua acted well in killing the people of Jericho since he still had the whole country to conquer and did not have time to spend on prisoners of war.
> It was right for him to act like this, since the conqueror has the right to do with the conquered villages as he pleases.
> They did not act well, but God told them and they had to follow his command. It was not right that they killed everyone.
> Joshua acted wrong in killing the people of Jericho. Why are the women and the children guilty? It is cruel to kill the old and weak and burn cities which thousands laboured to build.
> I do not think the Israeli army has to act in this manner since the Arabs are flesh and blood just like we are.
> I do not think the army has to act like Joshua as the Jews are already settled on the land.

This research caused an uproar at the time because academic authorities refused to publish it. Though Tel-Aviv University refused to publish, it was read out at a meeting of the Israeli Psychological Society in November 1963. Parts were published by the daily *Ha'aretz* and it was the publicity attracted by this action that created the uproar. Anyone familiar with Israeli reality knows that this research reveals almost standard attitudes of young children in Israel. In a country like Israel, where the Ministry of Education is in direct control of the education system, such views among young children are the direct product of the educational policy.

Advocates of the kibbutz type of communal settlement in Israel might wonder whether the kibbutz-born generation shares a similar morality to that revealed by the Tamarin research, or whether the socialist values of the parents have produced a different view. An answer to this question is provided by the discussion in *The Seventh Day*.[12] The book is based on discussion with kibbutz-born youngsters who fought in the June 1967 war. In a discussion on the future of the occupied territories we find the following:

> Hannan: One thing is clear to me, we won't go back to the old borders, at least not on the Golan heights.
>
> Avishai: I don't have any hard and fast ideas about it, because I think that what the Arabs on the West Bank think will be quite decisive. And that is not a small number – there are nearly a million. I am not a racist but I know one thing: I read the statistics and for every thousand Arabs in the country there are sixty births as compared to twenty among the same number of Jews. [They will be the majority]
>
> You can make a simple calculation that within one generation [the Arabs will outnumber the Jews] – and that is worrying ... The kibbutz is nothing to go by, today, in the cities, two children per family is the fashion. Okay, I say, very nice so we'll have a bi-national state, but we should be the majority, otherwise it won't be a Jewish state.[13]

The biography of this speaker reads: 'Age 22. Unmarried. Grandchild of two of the founding members of the kibbutz. Paratrooper. Fought in Jerusalem and the Golan Heights in 1967.' This is a youth of the third generation, reared in a militantly atheist atmosphere, without a shred of belief in religion, never discriminated against by anti-semites, yet deeply concerned about maintaining a non-religious, Jewish, identity, and haunted by the same fear as that expressed by Mrs Meir in Parliament. This is not fear of physical extermination.

It is quite clear by now that Israeli politics – like the whole of political Zionism – are deeply influenced by an identity complex. The political movement, which started by ignoring this complex, developed into an attempt to solve it, by basing the Jewishness of Israel on institutionalised ethnic discrimination. The adherents of this solution entangled themselves in a 'destiny' of perpetual conflict with the dispossessed Palestinians whom they subject, as a matter of principle, to eternal ethnic discrimination, barring them from sharing rights the Jews enjoy. This is bound to have repercussions on the Jewish culture itself.

Secular morals are an uneasy marriage of two conflicting moral codes. One is a universalist morality which is opposed to any discrimination between human beings, the other is a particularist morality based on discrimination between Jew and non-Jew. Some take pride in upholding both moral codes, insisting that they are merely different aspects of a single value system. Those conditioned by this code must choose which one to uphold during a conflict with non-Jews. Either one upholds the same moral considerations when dealing with the Palestinians as one does when dealing with Jews, or one does not. A choice between the two is inescapable.

Whatever the choice, it is always vehemently denounced either as a betrayal (of ethnic loyalty) or as hypocrisy by those who made the opposite choice. As this conflict is never overcome, and emerges anew with every generation, one is forced to conclude that it is a manifestation of a genuinely schizoid culture. However, the delicate balance between conflicting moralities is easily upset by external circumstances. The continuous conflict with the Palestinians tips the balance sharply against the universalist morality.

The spokesman of cultural Zionism, A'had Ha'am, was well aware of this possibility and commented, in 1898, on the very aim of political Zionism:

> ... such a Jewish State will be a fatal poison to our people, and will grind its spirit in the dust. Unable to become a political force to be proud of and unaware of its inner moral strength it will produce a tiny state which will be like a ball to its bigger neighbours and will exist only by diplomatic intrigues and perpetual subordination to those who dominate the area. This will not fill its spirit with ethnic dignity, whereas its culture in which it could find such dignity would not be rooted in such a state and not lived by. And thus it will be, much more than now, a debased small people, a slave in spirit to greater forces, envious of the 'fists' of its neighbours, and all its existence as a State owner will not add a dignified chapter to its history. Would it not be more dignified for an ancient people such as this, which has enlightened many nations, to disappear from history without reaching such a final chapter.[14]

This sad chapter prophesied by A'had Ha'am has already been written and, as he foresaw many years ago, has considerably reshaped the Jewish culture. Even such an essential element as the Jewish self-image has already been affected. In a recent meeting between 20 establishment writers (most of them of the second generation) and Mrs Meir, a meeting called at the request of the writers to protest against the refusal of the government to allow the Palestinian inhabitants of the Bar'am village, who are Israeli citizens, to return to their village after an exile of 20 years, one of the writers said: 'Justice has been thwarted, the villagers of Bar'am and Ikrit are left naked with their just demands. I believed all those years in the purity of our cause. It is impermissible that our self-image should change.'[15]

The secular Jewish self-image of moral righteousness cannot be maintained forever in a reality which consists of dispossessing the Palestinians, of ignoring their human, civil, and political rights. Political Zionism has produced a third generation wherein the majority has a personality structure closer to that of the Afrikaner than that of the European Jew. The self-image of such a person is not one of moral righteousness but one of a historical destiny. Indeed, the most virulent nationalistic passages from the Old Testament now serve as rationalisations to purge every shred of universal morality. The transformation from minority to majority has been successfully accomplished by Zionism. Is the result positive? If we accept the criterion of a significant Zionist figure, Dr Haim Weizman, Israel's first president, the answer is negative. Weizman states in his biography *Trial and Error*: 'History will judge the Jewish State according to its attitudes towards the Palestinians'. No need to wait for a verdict.

Notes and References

1. First published in *ISRACA*, No. 5, January 1973.
2. I distinguish between political, cultural, and emotional Zionism. The first aims to maintain a secular Jewish state, the second aspires to a cultural revival, the third is a sentiment which demands no action.
3. For example, the Shabtai Tsvi movement in the seventeenth century.
4. By 'culture' I mean here the totality of values, motives and aspirations which lend coherence and meaning to the existence of a particular society and its members.
5. By 'fossil' I mean an entity which neither develops nor degenerates.
6. Later, in the 1930s, Zionist leaders like Ben-Gurion were unwilling to share the efforts of evacuating Jews from Germany to countries other than Palestine. The Zionist movement is willing to help only those Jewish refugees who are willing to come to the Jewish state.
7. There is no civil marriage in Israel. Jewish, Muslim, and Christian marriages must be performed according to the appropriate religious ruling.
8. Most secular Israelis reject the notion of 'Israeli ethnicity', insisting that they are Jews ethnically, Israelis by citizenship, and non-believers.
9. *Knesset Debates*, official publication, Jerusalem, vol. 13, p. 770, debate of 9 February 1970.
10. By 'generation' I do not mean an age-group, but a group which shares a common social experience and mentality.
11. *Jerusalem Post*, 30 September 1968. Apart from the last statement, most of Dayan's speech is a quote from Dr A. Rupin, a prominent Zionist leader in the 1930s.
12. *The Seventh Day*, 1971, London: Penguin Books.

13. *The Seventh Day*, p. 143.
14. *The Jewish Problem and the Jewish State, Collected Works of A'had Ha'am,* Hebrew edition, 1898, p. 135.
15. Yedioth Ahararoth, 3 August 1972.

4

Israeliness

In order to reduce the misunderstanding that the following essay is bound to produce I want to emphasise here that by 'Israeliness' I do not mean the legal status of being a citizen of the state of Israel, or the holding of an Israeli passport. The 'Israeliness' to which I refer is a cultural entity, a set of attitudes, a state of mind which shapes the responses of a particular group of people.

Just as 'being British' describes a set of attitudes, a particular mentality, so too does 'Israeliness'. This mentality is shared by many Israeli citizens, but not by all. There are Israeli citizens who do not have the mentality of 'Israeliness', for example all the Palestinian Arabs who are Israeli citizens. They are of course Arabs, and share attitudes and a cultural background common to all Arabs even though the particular circumstances of their life in Palestine have produced some attitudes which are unique to them. There is nothing surprising in this; however, some readers may find it surprising that not even all the Jewish citizens of Israel share the attitudes of 'Israeliness'. Anyone who has doubts on this point need only pay a visit to the Jewish religious quarter of Meah-She'arim in Jerusalem and try to establish some contact with the Orthodox, religious Jews wearing the black robes and black, or fur, hats. These people are certainly Jews, usually also Israeli citizens, but their attitudes qualify for the title of 'Orthodox Judaism', not for 'Israeliness'. They themselves would insist on this distinction. They will not deny that 'Israeliness' exists, but for them it is an abomination, sheer blasphemy, which they abhor. They consider their attitudes to be Jewish rather than Israeli.

In May 1993 the religious SHAS Party threatened to leave the coalition government unless the Minister of Education, the liberal Ms Shulamit Aloni, be removed from her post as Minister of Education. During this Cabinet crisis a popular daily published the following article expressing the response of 'Israeliness':

We are at War, by Yair Lapid

We are at war, but we are unwilling to admit it. We'll tell ourselves everything but the truth. It's not because of the police investigation [of the Minister of the Interior, Rabbi J. Der'ee of SHAS], nor because of the budget, nor because of 'El Ha'ma'yan' [a religious foundation which received funds illegally from Der'ee]. It is due to the [cultural] war. For many years it was said that the day peace starts, the conflict between atheists and religious will erupt in full force. Now peace is on the horizon and the war started. This is not a coalition squabble, this is the rearguard battle of the Israeli culture. I take Minister Der'ee [of SHAS], and Rabbi Ovadia Yosef [leader of SHAS Party] seriously. They genuinely and sincerely believe there is no place in our culture for Darwin, Freud, Einstein. They want to uproot Chagall, Beethoven, and Hemingway from our culture. They are afraid of Shakespeare, the Beatles, jeans and cable TV. They consider themselves God's messengers and, like all fanatics, will never stop. They will take bite after bite from our view of the world. Their list is long, and everybody is in it. They won't rest in their mission as long as Kafka, Michelangelo, Alterman and Mick Jagger exist in our culture. We are at war. But only one side is fighting. There is something pathetic and sad in the lack of will of the atheists to defend themselves. The orthodox present us with ritualistic righteousness, accuse us of being pagan, and threaten to drag us into the kind of cultural ghetto from which we escaped. We could have levelled against them the most modern weapons of the mental battlefield, pluralism, freedom of choice and knowledge, and democracy in its deepest sense. Had we conducted this war as we ought to, even God would have come to the rescue. Instead, Rabin goes to Kanossa and Aloni goes home. We are at war, and at the moment the orthodox are winning.[1]

It seems that the cultural conflict between Israeli and Judaic attitudes, submerged because of the political conflict with the Arabs, is about to surface again. Non-religious Israeliness is not neutral in this conflict; occasionally it has a bash at religious Judaism, as did the poetess Yona Wallach in the early 1980s in her poem 'Tefilin'. She refers to the leather straps which an Orthodox Jew wraps around his left hand during the morning prayer ('Tefila' means prayer).

TEFILIN
Yona Wallach

Come to me
don't let me do a thing
you'll do for me
everything you'll do for me
anything I'll start doing
you'll do for me

I'll lay Tefilin
pray
you'll lay the Tefilin for me
wrap them round my arms
play them on me
pass them gently over my body
rub them well into me
arouse me all over
make me faint with ecstasy
pass them over my clitoris
tie them around my waist
make me come faster
play them on me
tie my hands and feet
do things to me
against my will
turn me on my belly
put Tefilin like a bit between my teeth
ride me like a mare
pull my head back
till I scream with pain
and you have had your fill
then I'll pass them over your body
with an unveiled intention on my face
Oh how cruel my face will be
I'll pass them slowly over your body
slow slow slow
I'll wrap them around your neck
I'll wrap them a few times round your neck, on one side
and on the other I'll tie them to something stable
very heavy, maybe rotating
I'll pull and pull
until your soul departs
until I choke you
completely with Tefilin
stretching along the stage
and into the stunned audience.

This poem created an uproar among Orthodox Jews when it was first published, but many atheist Israelis support its outspoken rejection of religious values and practices they consider to be archaic superstition.

Jewish attitudes are always linked to the Jewish religion whereas Israeliness is atheist, modern, and, at best, linked to Jewish traditions, not to the belief or practice of the religion.

The substance of Israeliness is the use of Hebrew as a mother tongue at home, plus atheism, modernity, lack of minority complexes, and the experience of a non-religious education in Israel at least between the ages of 6 and 16.

Most Jewish immigrants in Israel who arrived after finishing their primary and secondary education elsewhere do not acquire the mentality I label 'Israeliness'. Those who got their primary and secondary schooling in a secular school in Israel acquired 'Israeliness' there. It is very rare for people who emigrated to Israel after finishing high school elsewhere to acquire 'Israeliness'. Such people, even if they use Hebrew at home, were shaped by formative experiences which in turn produce attitudes that distinguish them from Israeliness. I am not claiming superiority or inferiority of Israeliness *vis-à-vis* Judaism or Diaspora Jewishness. I only claim that there are qualitatively differences between these three mentalities. These are three, different, mutually exclusive cultural worlds. Their existence constitutes the historical process, during the last two centuries, of the fragmentation of the Jewish group identity.

Israeliness is neither Judaism nor Jewishness. Each of these three states of mind is in conflict with the other two.

Israeliness is the local nationalism of the 'Hebrew-speaking Gentiles' in Israel.

Jewishness is the ethnocentrism of Diaspora Jews.

Judaism is the theocentric mentality of religious Jews.

Prime Minister Rabin is an example of a person with Israeli, rather than Jewish, attitudes. If he wears a skullcap while attending a religious ceremony he does it for the sake of his hosts, not due to his religious beliefs. On the other hand Prime Ministers like Ben-Gurion, Meir, Begin and Shamir lacked 'Israeliness', and denounced its very existence. They shared the mentality I label 'secular Diaspora Jewishness'. The main difference between 'secular Diaspora Jewishness' and Israeliness is that the former is afflicted by the psychological complexes of a minority within a non-Jewish host society, whereas Israeliness is free of minority complexes. Israelis have a *de facto* identity coherent with their social experience. This is something Diaspora Jews lack; they feel alienated from some attitudes of the host society and often have superiority/inferiority attitudes *vis-à-vis* non-Jews. Israeliness is tainted by provinciality but not by a minority complex.

The idea that Israeliness exists but differs from Jewishness is a frightening anathema for many Jews, and for Zionists in particular. The reason is simple: Zionism is the idea that all the Jews in the world constitute one nation whose homeland is Zion (the biblical name for Palestine). Any suggestion that a schism exists between Jewish believers and non-believers, or between Diaspora Jews and Israelis, is abhorrent to Jewish nationalists. These nationalists worship an idol – the Jewish nation. The possibility that this idol is irreparably fragmented, and that the creation of Israel accelerated the fragmentation process, outrages the Zionists. It is for this reason that the existence of Israeliness is denied or shrouded in a cloud of confusion by Zionists. In the 1950s the Israeli government became aware that young, atheistic Israelis had developed a non-Jewish mentality. The government tried to overcome this by introducing special lessons on 'Jewish consciousness' into the secular schools. The lessons consisted mainly of presenting Jewish history as a history of persecution. In the 1980s a religious Minister of Education introduced organised school tours from Israel to Nazi extermination camps in Poland to boost 'Jewish conscious-ness'. The idea was that those who no longer practise the religion will lose the Jewish identity, but as long as others persecute them because of their Jewish origin they are forced to accept it. Ms Shulamit Aloni, who became Minister of Education in 1992, went to Poland in April 1993 to celebrate the fiftieth anniversary of the Jewish uprising in the Warsaw ghetto. On this occasion she met Israeli high school pupils who told her about their impressions from a recent visit to Auschwitz and Maidanek. Some of these views were quoted in the Israeli daily *Hadashot*. One boy, Leeran Avishar, said:

> Facing all these atrocities stirs one's humanity, you develop a will to do good to people. I didn't think only about Jews, it is universal, this feeling. Even after my emotions calm down there will remain the memory and knowledge that we must not forget, that we must be human, as one human being to another, that things like this must not be allowed to happen. Not only in this country but in the whole world. In such a tour you suddenly identify also with Judaism. I am not Jewish, but during the visit to Poland I went to a synagogue and prayed. I said 'Hark Israel', 'Kadish'. I always heard it but until now I never paid attention to what it said ... I finished by saying I am proud to be Jewish, and I am proud that a nation which was exterminated managed to create a State as we did. I thought we are in agreement but she [Ms Aloni] didn't like what I said. I said I am proud to show the flag here. There's a difference between pride and arrogance ... She said something very true; to be free is a natural right, I don't have to come to Poland to prove that I am free. I never felt inferior. I felt natural with this. But when you see these atrocities, and absorb this, you feel the need to raise the flag high and say 'I am here'.

Another boy, Moti Israeli, added:

> ... Before I went to Poland I thought about the people, I wanted to understand if this is human at all. It seemed irrational to me that people will do this to other people. Crematoria, gas chambers, hats, shoes, artificial limbs, lists of all possessions of

these people which were taken from them together with their lives. Until I came here I found it hard to believe. But when I saw it I felt very uncomfortable. I thought that just as we hate the Arabs so did the Germans hate us, and look what it came to. I didn't moderate my views, on the contrary. Last elections I supported 'Zomet' and now I support the transfer [of the Palestinians to Arab countries]. Jews in Europe were allowed to flee but no one accepted them. If in our region the Arabs will be accepted there will be less dead. We have had the Intifada for so many years, and so many dead, ours and theirs. We must put them into Saudi Arabia and stop worrying about them. The Nazis knew nobody will accept the Jews, but we are much more humane than them: the Arabs have a place to go to, let them go to Arafat. We live in the promised land, the Nazis had no proof they were promised their land. We have the Bible, this is the proof. I do not think we shall do to the Arabs what the Nazis did to the Jews. Throw them out? Yes. Exterminate? No.[2]

The confusion is enormous. Leeran says 'I am not Jewish but during the visit I went to a synagogue and prayed' and later adds 'I am proud to be Jewish'. Moti, who is also non-religious, is worried about the implications of ethnic hatred and apologises for Israeli policies towards the Palestinians by using the Bible as proof to his right over Palestine. The visit, organised by the Ministry of Education on the initiative of a zealous religious former Minister (Zevulun Hamer) achieved its aim. Israeli youth which before the visit did not feel itself to be Jewish now feels linked to a history of persecution. It acquires a negative substitute for the positive religious definition of Jewishness which it lacks, namely: 'I may not have a clear idea what secular Jewishness means, but as long as I am persecuted by Jew-haters I am a Jew.' None of these Israeli kids was personally persecuted as a Jew ... but they now identify with the Zionist version of Jewish history, namely that Jews were always persecuted because of their origin – and will always be – and therefore need a state of their own to protect them from persecution. In May 1993, when Israel–Arab peace negotiations were resumed in Washington and Israel signalled its readiness to hand back the Golan Heights to Syria, someone scribbled a graffito above the motorway near Tel-Aviv saying: 'ONCE ALL THE WORLD WAS AGAINST US, NOW IT'S THE [Israeli] GOVERNMENT AS WELL'. This expresses neither a Judaic view nor an Israeli one; it is typically Zionist. Some people might argue that Nazi extermination of six million Jews was bound to produce such attitudes among Jews. This argument fails to account for the fact that Orthodox religious Jews never acquired this 'history of persecution' version despite the fact that they too were exterminated by the Nazis. They have a positive, religious definition of their identity and history.

To an impartial observer it would seem obvious that a population sharing geographical, political, social and spiritual conditions that are totally different from those shared by Diaspora Jews will be influenced by the new conditions and develop a new mentality. However, since the political leadership of this population considers such mentality as heresy, and combats it by denying its existence, the inevitable outcome is confusion. This confusion is increased by the psychological need of many non-believers of Jewish background to insist they are still Jewish despite the fact that they no longer uphold the original faith. The confusion is transmitted to the new generation by parents, teachers, writers and political leaders. No one ventures to clear up the confusion, either because they are themselves confused, or because they fear to expose the painful truth about the unbridgeable differences between hostile segments of a society which is supposed to be one unit.

Young non-believers in Israel, whose attitudes are definitely Israeli (rather than Jewish), have difficulty deciding on their cultural identity. They are told they are Jews but they don't practise the 613 rules and are not clear what Jewishness means. They are told that Israeliness doesn't exist. They are never presented with a clear definition of either. Their parents and their cultural and political leaders lack clear, generally accepted definitions. This fuzziness in defining one's own cultural identity persists among the 80 per cent who no longer practise the 613 rules.

The notion that Jews consist of an ethnic entity, a nation, even when they no longer believe or practise their religion, creates a need for a secular definition of this ethnicity. No generally accepted definition exists. *There is no secular definition of Jewishness.* Any new definition will be in conflict with the 'mitsvot' one which is accepted by all as legitimate. Any new definition will always lack legitimacy while upholders of the legitimate definition exist and deny the legitimacy of any other definition. Individuals produce private definitions which are immediately contested by others. The quest for a generally accepted secular definition of Jewish ethnicity is the psychological source of Zionism. Only people who have this need are candidates for Zionism. Zionism insists that Jews are an ethnic group quite apart from their religion. Zionists preach loyalty to the Jewish nation as a substitute for loyalty to the Jewish God. Some pledge loyalty to the Jewish state, Zion.

What – apart from religion – makes this nation specifically Jewish? To this question Zionists have no generally accepted answer, and whatever answer they give raises controversy among Jews. Most Israelis grasp the state of Israel as the core of their ethnic identity rather than as an instrument for regulating the life of the citizens. The Zionist organisation spreads its view among Jews everywhere that loyalty to the state of Israel is the core of Jewishness.

This was never true in the past and is not true today. Those who practise daily the 613 religious rules were known to themselves and to others as 'Jews' for centuries while no Jewish state existed. No wonder they vehemently reject this view. Loyalty to the State of Israel is not the core of their identity. Loyalty to the Jewish God is. They have no shred of doubt they are Jewish. They worship neither the Jewish state nor the Jewish nation. They consider both as idol worship. Are they wrong? Secular Jewish ethnicity is as solid as the smile of the Cheshire cat in *Alice in Wonderland*.

All non-believers who insist on their Jewishness have identity problems that they try to overcome in one way or another. Those born in Israel, who are atheists with Hebrew as mother tongue and who received their primary and secondary education in Israel, have a *de facto* Israeli identity different from that of a Diaspora Jewish identity or from a religious identity. This identity can be labelled 'Israeliness'. It is not recognised *de jure* because such recognition would admit the existence of a cultural gap between Israeliness and Jewishness, thus undermining the Zionist view that all Jews in the world constitute a single ethnic entity. In the late 1940s and early 1950s, a group of Israeli intellectuals drew attention to the cultural gap between Israeliness and Jewishness. They suggested that Israeliness can be taken as a continuation of the cultural traditions of the ancient Israelites who lived in Palestine in biblical times, whereas Jewishness is a product of life as a dispersed group in exile. These intellectuals were labelled 'Cana'anites' (after the original name of Palestine ('Cana'an') in biblical times). They used the term 'Hebrew' to denote secular Israeli cultural identity. In their manifesto, published in 1945, they declared:

> Anyone who is not a son of this land, the land of the Hebrews, cannot be a Hebrew, is not a Hebrew, and never was a Hebrew. Anyone who comes from the Diaspora is a Jew, not a Hebrew, and can be nothing but a Jew. The Jew and the Hebrew can never be identical. He who is a Hebrew cannot be a Jew, and he who is a Jew cannot be a Hebrew. A son of a nation cannot belong to a religious community which considers that nation to be a religious community.

This was the first assertion of the unbridgeable cultural gap between Jewishness and Israeliness. At the time this declaration drew vehement denunciation from the vast majority of Jews in Palestine. Today many will accept it as a description of sociological reality. There is no need nowadays to legitimise Israeliness by trying to connect it with some mythical ancient Cana'anite culture in biblical times. Modern Israel, with TV, rock 'n' roll, Aids and nuclear weapons, is too remote from biblical times to make any cultural connection meaningful. Instead, the observation that Israelis are

'*Hebrew-speaking gentiles*' is much more to the point. Indeed, most Israelis who live for any length of time outside Israel find more in common with local gentiles than with local Jews. They do not share the sensitivities of the local Jews as a cultural minority. They have a clear notion of the difference between themselves and the locals but are not troubled by it. Local, non-religious Jews feel the difference, but lacking a clear, indisputable definition of their own identity, feel threatened by it. Anyone trying to understand Israeli society must take into account the emerging, and constantly growing, Israeli ethnicity. Eventually Israel will be the state of the Israelis, not of the Jews. In this respect the difference between Israeliness and Jewishness has similarities to the difference between Dutch and Afrikaaner cultures. In both cases a group from the original culture branched out into a colonising enterprise and became shaped by it. The differences from the mother culture grow ever wider with time although at first there is a reluctance to admit this. Gradually the two cultures drift apart, and the gulf between them increases till finally they separate completely.

The persistent efforts by Israeli authorities (who are still dominated by Zionist ideology) to combat and deny the existence of Israeliness must not be allowed to blur the issue. Lack of a clear distinction between Israeliness and Jewishness adds confusion to political and to cultural issues. Israeliness has distinct economic and political concerns which differ from those of Zionism. It is concerned not with world Jewry but with people who live in Israel. Israeliness is the local nationalism of people born and bred in Israel. Zionism is the secular nationalism of Diaspora Jewry. Diaspora secular Jewry suffers from an insecurity concerning its identity and depends on persecution for defining its group identity. Israeliness has a solid sense of its identity and does not feel threatened by non-Jewish cultures. Israeliness is not averse to employment of Arabs in the Israeli economy. It has no religious obsession with sovereignty over every inch of the soil between the river Jordan and the Mediterranean sea. Israelis who hold such views are motivated by security considerations, not by religious ones. Israeliness is aware that living in the Middle East requires a *modus vivendi* with the surrounding Arab world, necessitating territorial compromises with the Palestinians. When Israeliness and its separation from Jewishness is recognised (by Jews and non-Jews alike) and taken into account in political considerations, it will be a step towards overcoming strife in Palestine.

Notes and References

1. *Ma'ariv*, literary supplement, 14 May 1993.
2. *Hadashot*, weekend supplement, 23 April 1993.

5

Twenty-six Years Later (1990)

C.L.R. James once said to me that one has to observe a society for at least two or three decades before one can get an idea in which direction it is moving. He meant something similar to discerning a long-term trend in statistics. It takes time to separate the short-term fluctuations from the long-term trend. Only after such a separation can the more permanent features be distinguished from the transient ones.

A friend suggested that I write down my observations on the long-term changes I discerned in Israel after spending 26 years abroad.

The first change I noticed when I recently discussed politics in Israel is that humanism (the principle that all human beings, whatever the differences between them, must be treated as equals), which was an assumption taken for granted by most Israelis up to 1967, is now upheld by only a minority. Most Jews in 1990 (probably even a decade earlier) take it for granted that every ethnic group is justified in giving preferential treatment to its own members. In other words, nationalism – even racism – gained a legitimacy. If you accused anyone in Israel in 1964 of racism they would reply, indignantly, 'how dare you?', whereas in 1990 such accusation often solicits the response: 'what's wrong with putting your own people first?' There is little purpose in continuing an argument after such comment because there is no common ground between nationalism and humanism. In other words, humanist assumptions are now upheld only by a small minority, whereas the majority upholds nationalism. The 'Likud' followers are extreme nationalists, whereas Labour followers are moderate nationalists.

When the racist Rabbi Meir Kahana was assassinated in New York, Prime Minister Shamir declared: 'This is a direct blow to the heart of the Jewish people.'

Some heart. It seems as if Israel has had a heart transplant while I've been away.

Every one of the wars (1967, 1973, 1982) shifted public opinion and the political spectrum further towards extreme nationalism, leaving behind small residues of former co-thinkers. Anyone upholding humanist views nowadays is ridiculed as a 'beautiful soul', meaning a sucker, who doesn't know what life is really all about.

Despite the fact that the Israeli army today is larger and better equipped than ever before, the sense of personal security is worse than it has ever been. Most people have installed special locks on their doors, not just against burglars but against PLO attacks. Many Israeli Jews carry private guns, something unheard of before 1967. There is a glaring paradox comparing the military might of the state with the individual sense of insecurity.

A second, immediately noticeable change is the sharp shift towards religion. In 1964 it was rare to see people wearing skullcaps. Some believers would take their skullcap off when entering their place of work. Very few wore them in the army. Nowadays there are a lot of skullcaps around, even among soldiers, bank clerks, teachers, doctors, etc. Although the majority of Israeli Jews do not observe religious rules – they drive their cars on Saturdays, and eat non-Kosher – most of them nowadays will fast on Yom Kippur and refrain from driving their cars on that day. In 1964 Yom Kippur was ignored by the secular majority. The stunning victory in the 1967 war, when the Israeli public expected defeat, drove many to believe in divine miracles. A considerable number of public figures, actors, writers, musicians, who were formerly on the left, 'saw the light' and became religious.

This was accelerated by the general decline in Israeli social democracy, whose authority, economic power and ideology has been declining ever since the war of 1973.

In 1964 the elite consisted of politicians like Ben-Gurion, or Golda Meir, who owned neither a house nor a car, academics who were totally devoted to their subject and had a miserable income, or members of the kibbutzim, who tilled the land for no profit. All these people were dedicated to the creation of a 'just society', and people were valued according to their contribution to this goal. Anyone suspected of pursuing personal interests was 'out'. The few who had money refrained from showing it. School leavers were concerned with how best they could serve the nation. All this has changed drastically. Nowadays money talks. The rich constitute the elite; wealth is flaunted and envied. The central aim of most Israeli Jews today is how to make a lot of money, by hook or by crook, and get away with it. Money has changed from a means into an end in itself. Even members of the kibbutzim now demand wages.

In 1964 anyone who left a kibbutz – or the country – was considered a traitor, nowadays the leavers are envied by those left behind. When maximising personal profit becomes respectable every other ideology, including nationalism, is under threat.

There are noticeable changes in the social domain. The oriental Jews, who immigrated in the 1950s (from the Arab countries) and were totally subordinated to the European elite which produced Zionism and Israel, brought forth a new generation, born and bred in Israel, which forms a majority in the Jewish population. This new generation no longer feels subordinated to the European elite or to its parents. Some of this generation have travelled abroad and are familiar with the modern world. Every political party panders to this group. In the past their votes could be bought en bloc, by pandering to heads of families, clans, congregations; nowadays this is no longer the case. They have become much more individually minded.

There are other post-60s oddities. Single-parent families, and health-food shops, were non-existent, even unimaginable, in 1964. Today they are a common feature and attract no attention; so too the large number of latest-model Mercedes and BMWs on the roads – their numbers exceed what I saw in London. Pollution is a major issue. The beautiful Mediterranean beaches, as well as the fresh-water resources, are often polluted. The beaches, as well as the roads, cities, even villages, are far more crowded than I remember. The country's Jewish population has more than doubled in my absence.

The beautiful beach of Saidna-Ali, with its clean white sand and clear water, where I used to swim, had rarely more than a dozen bathers. Nowadays you can't find a place in the car park on summer Saturdays. The sand is littered with plastic bottles, the sea discoloured by untreated effluent from the new hotels and munitions work nearby. The beach is overcrowded. The Muslim mosque, which gave its name to the beach, is in disrepair, and its cemetery has become a rubbish dump. This is typical rather than exceptional of many former natural beauty spots throughout the country.

High-rise hotels and luxury apartment blocks abound in Tel-Aviv, Haifa, even Jerusalem. When I left there was not a single building taller than six stories in the entire country.

There is a visible trend of Americanisation in the cultural, economic and social domain. In the 1950s and 1960s, when Israel was ruled by the Zionist Labour movement, it emulated the social policies of the British Labour Party – concepts like 'wage freeze', 'package deal', 'purchase tax', 'value added tax', were copied from Britain and became part of Israeli life. From the 1970s onwards the American way of life has become the model. Unemployment, hitherto almost unknown, is threatening many wage earners, including academics. Privatisation is the name of the game. It is pathetic to see Israeli managers, even of kibbutz industries, swinging their James Bond cases like brokers on Wall Street. They emulate an appearance not economic power. *Dallas* and *Dynasty* are smash hits on Israeli TV whereas until the 1960s they would have been considered despicable.

I used to look down on the quality of Israeli-made goods and preferred foreign ones, but nowadays I find the quality and design of many Israeli products excellent. There are many innovative products for sale and more local high technology on the consumer market than I expected. When I left, citrus fruit was a major export, nowadays it has been superseded by hi-tech goods. Israel produces body scanners, pilotless planes, guidance systems for missiles, genetically manipulated seeds for special crops, desalination plants, glycol, a large spectrum of pharmaceutics, and many hi-tech goods. It is a pity that the natural market for the Israeli industry, the Arab world, remains closed due to the political conflict. Both sides could gain tremendously from an economic-industrial-scientific co-operation, forming the common market of the Middle East.

Clearly, many of the trends described here are a result of Israel's conflict with the Palestinians and its relation to the Arab world. My view was, and remains, that the Israeli society and economy are small, and lack mass and inertia. Unlike a massive society numbering many millions like, say, the Arab world, they depend heavily on external influences. One can say that Israeli economy and society can be steered around like a small sailing boat whereas a country like Egypt, where 1 million babies are added to the population every eight months, is constrained by its size and forced to follow a discernible trend – it cannot be steered around like Israeli society. I hope Israel is steered around before it is too late.

Living in another country gives you an outside view of the country you were formerly inside, as well as a new social and political environment to compare with the old one.

One of the first peculiarities I became aware of on my return was the strong, ubiquitous element of emotional blackmail employed by Israelis in every political discussion. Cynics expect such blackmail to be exercised by Israeli leaders on Western public opinion and political leadership ('you caused the Holocaust, and refrained from saving us from it, therefore you have no right to criticise us'), but I saw it exercised by every Israeli political party against its rivals and opponents in Israel, often by people within the same party, and by individuals upon themselves. This happens when a person runs out of rational arguments but refuses to accept that his/her assumptions are wrong. They switch to emotionalism to drown their own rationality. The point is difficult to demonstrate because it is expressed not by verbal statement but by intonation. One way to describe it to people in the UK is as follows: fetch from your memory the TV image of Reverend Ian Paisley giving a public speech in Belfast. Remember the intonations and facial expressions? Now imagine an ordinary person in the street in Tel-Aviv during a discussion of Israeli politics suddenly lapsing into the same into-nations and facial expressions. When this happens you know they have switched into emotional self-blackmail. They have run out of rational arguments but rather than admit the validity of their opponent's arguments they work themselves into this self-righteous rage. My advice is: don't fall for the act, stick to your guns, don't apologise, and don't walk away. When there is a lull in the tirade repeat your arguments quietly and look your adversary in the eye. Whether they resort to violence or walk away, in either case you've won.

The second point that drew my attention was the Israelis' attitude towards their state. Most Israelis personalise the state. They talk about Israel as if it were a person. Expressions like 'the state has promised' or 'the state has said' abound. I've never come across anything similar in Britain, France or the USA. On one occasion, when an Israeli said to me: 'but the state has signed a document,' and I asked: 'with which hand?', the person was aghast. Israelis rarely think of their state as a bureaucratic apparatus of elected representatives and administrative staff whose job it is to shape and implement policies. My view is that this is a by-product of the psychological role of Israel, as the core of secular Jewish identity – a role similar to the nucleus of a (chemical) crystallisation process. It is a core around which the nebulous notions of secular Jewishness can crystallise. The fact that 'secular' and 'Jewish' are contradictory is papered over – for the time being – by the existence of a state which is both 'Jewish' and secular. Most Israelis identify their image – and self-image – with that of their state. Many are horrified by the atrocities committed against the Palestinians (the large number of Palestinian children killed by the Israeli army) because this damages Israel's image abroad. 'What will the world think of us?' is far more common than 'How can we do this to another human being?'

As far as attitudes to Arabs are concerned, most Israelis will admit that Arabs are also human beings, but they lack emotional sensitivity to this fact. If a Jewish five-year-old is killed by an Arab most Jews will be moved emotionally and the entire Jewish public will be outraged, but if an Arab five-year-old is shot by an Israeli soldier (at least a dozen were) only a few Israeli Jews will protest. The majority will remain unmoved emotionally. Most of those who will protest care more about the damage to Israel's (and their own) image than about the wasting of a young life or the grieving family. This lack of emotional sensitivity to the suffering of non-Jews produces an inability to project one's own motivations on to others. Israel will protest about the killing of a Jew in, say, Paris, but they cannot comprehend why Palestinians in the Gaza strip demonstrate and protest ('riot' in Israeli parlance) about the killing of 21 Muslim worshippers on Temple Mount by the Israeli police.

A third point I became aware of was the total inability of most Israelis to see society as a system of roles. For most Israelis there is no separation of actor from act. They identify totally with their social roles. The notion of an independent personality is, by and large, missing. Most Israelis are so involved in what they do that they become what they do. They cannot imagine a different possibility. Anyone familiar with Israelis' roles can predict their behaviour and responses. Visiting a kibbutz I felt I was walking among marionettes activated by computer programmes with which I was familiar. I could predict the phrases they would use to respond to my questions, and even their intonations and facial expressions. This occurred again and again, on meeting soldiers, farmers, journalists, doctors, even academics.

In Britain, with its strong structure of social classes shaping a set of clearly defined, easily recognisable social roles, I often came across people in all classes who were fully aware that they were playing a particular social role but who had at the same time a personality independent of that role. Personalities like this are mentally alive. In Israel I found very few such people. The majority were going through the motions set by their conditioning without being aware of it.

Failure to distinguish between personality and role makes understanding otherness a problem. An Israeli friend who had lived for many years in London told me a true story about a leading Israeli politician (David Ha'Cohen) coming to London shortly after the 1956 Suez War. He wanted to explain Israel's reasons for starting that war to the British Labour Party which opposed the war. The Israeli Ambassador in London, Eliyahu Eilat, tried to dissuade Ha'Cohen from doing so, and advised him to 'let sleeping dogs sleep'. But Ha'Cohen insisted, and Eilat had to arrange a meeting with Hugh Gaitskell (Labour's leader). On returning from that meeting Ha'Cohen told Eilat: 'I explained our case to him, and he accepted our point of view.' Eilat, knowing that Labour has not changed its anti-Suez policies, was surprised and asked what exactly Gaitskell had said. Ha'Cohen replied: 'He said "I see your point".' For most Israelis this means 'I agree with you' – the possibility of understanding a viewpoint and disagreeing with it is unimaginable to most Israelis. In other words, sensitivity and respect for 'otherness' is lacking.

Many Israelis refuse to admit that their society – and politics – are the outcome of their decisions and choices. Cornered in a political discussion, they will argue: 'that decision' (to start a war, occupation, massacre, etc.) 'was imposed upon us, *we simply had no choice*'. This is a standard way to evade responsibility. When you choose between options you are responsible for the consequences of your choice; you could choose differently – say, not to annex half the territory the UN allocated to the Palestinians in the 1947 Partition, or not to attack Egypt on 29 October 1956, and again on 5 June 1967 ...

To refer to all these decisions in terms of 'we had no choice' is a mental necessity. There is an inability to face a situation to which blame may be attached. For most Israelis blame is always on the other side, whether that side is Arab, parent, child, spouse, friend, or the other driver. Many Israelis blame the Palestinians for atrocities committed by Israeli soldiers; 'I hate the Arabs for *forcing* our boys to behave like animals', is a common phrase. Who forces a soldier to shoot an unarmed demonstrator in the head?

Whatever the case, you are always OK; the other is to blame. Is this related to the fact that in Hebrew there is no distinction between 'blame' and 'guilt', the same word being used for both?

Always blaming others is an indicator of emotional immaturity, an inability to take a critical look at oneself and reach the conclusion that the blame rests on you. Most Israelis would conclude: 'If the blame rests on me then I am guilty.' The possibility that blame does not always imply guilt is beyond them. They find it impossible to admit either.

Another peculiar trait I became aware of is that Israelis tend to complain rather than get angry. In the music scene this is revealed by the fact that there is not a single Israeli rock band expressing anger – nothing like the Rolling Stones' 'Paint it Black', or the Sex Pistols' 'God Save the Queen'. Instead there is – at best – a whining, complaining tone expressing something like 'How can you do this to me?'

I find most Israeli popular music bands boring, either because they pander to the audience, trying to imitate European bands, or express complaint. There is not a single note expressing anger about an establishment that is responsible for at least three major wars (causing thousands of dead and disabled) and four decades of ongoing armed conflict with the Palestinians and the surrounding Arab states.

If you suggest to Israelis that their *governments* were responsible for the wars of 1956, 1967, 1982, most of them will respond angrily – 'We?'

6

Reply to a Letter, December 1993

Can *any* traditional cultural identity adapt to modern Western culture and retain its original character? My answer is 'No'. This issue has been troubling anthropologists for more than a century. The introduction of implements based on Western technology into traditional cultures brought about profound changes in these cultures. I include in this category all the native cultures of the Americas as well as those in Asia and Africa. They all want axes and knives whose edges stay sharp despite frequent use. They all want guns, matches, radios, cars, outboard engines, planes, TV, etc. What they do not realise is that these implements are physical embodiments of a culture whose test for the validity of everything is verification by repeatable practice. Whatever passes this test is accepted as valid; whatever fails it is considered myth or superstition. I am not passing a value judgement here. I am not saying good/bad because I'm fully aware that 'good' cannot be defined objectively. It may be that Western technology will greatly improve our biological existence but turn us into people afflicted by loneliness and depression. I say merely that traditional cultures addicted to Western technology lose their validity. They become qualitatively different from what they were. Western technology is a cultural Trojan horse, an agent of cultural change. I have seen this happen to bedouins in the Sinai Desert within the last 20 years. Until the 1970s they still cooked on fires of desert bushes, used camels for transport, lived in camelhair tents. They had no radios, cars or TVs. Rank within society was determined by descent, not by wealth. All this has disappeared within a mere 25 years. I remember returning from a night drive in Dahab in 1985 at 2 a.m. Passing through an encampment where the elders used to sit round a fire and tell stories, I noticed they were sitting round a TV set watching *Dallas*. Today many of them own cars. Egypt has introduced an electrical grid and there are iceboxes everywhere (they had none in 1980). They still speak their language, and the older generation stick to the old habits but the young emulate the West and look down on the traditional culture, its habits and beliefs. Their future generations will acquire all the assumptions, attitudes and expectations of Western civilisation. They will still be speaking Arabic and may retain the 700 different terms pertaining to camels, but what significance will all their cultural

60

tradition have for them? Merely the significance of folklore. It will no longer have its former validity as the only way of life worth living.

Can they still be labelled 'bedouins' after having absorbed the assumptions, expectations and attitudes of Western civilisation? Can the label 'bedouin', which signified a desert nomad living in camelhair tents, cooking on open fires, sipping coffee ground from beans roasted on that fire, travelling by camel, whose daughters graze goats, still be called 'bedouin' when he lives in a permanent stone structure, drives a car, cooks on gas, watches TV, sips Nescafé and thinks mostly about making money? Anyone can stick any label on anything, but is it justified to stick a label which has been used for centuries to denote item A, on to item B which differs qualitatively from item A?

My answer is an emphatic No! Anyone who does this is confusing him/herself and misleading others. It is usually done by people who find themselves caught between two cultural identities, neither of which they fully embrace. Such people are said to have a 'cultural roots problem'. They prefer to label themselves as a variant of their traditional cultural identity. Some cultural identities are not sharply defined and allow variations within certain limits. My view is that all those who share the assumptions, expectations and attitudes of Western culture differ qualitatively from any variant of their former traditional culture. If they keep insisting that they are still members of their traditional culture they become haunted by the need to redefine it because its original definition has lost its validity for them.

The new definitions never acquire the same legitimacy as the original definition of the culture. Adherents of the original definition will challenge the legitimacy of any new definition. This situation occurs all over the world. Those who use the name of the original culture to denote their new, changed version of it are attempting to paper over the gap between the two by using the same name for both.

The Jews are in the same boat as the Gypsies, Innuit, Yanoman, or Apachis.

How do most traditional cultures respond to this crisis? Their members split into three factions. The traditionalists try to isolate themselves and minimise contact with Western civilisation. The Amish forbid their members the use of cars, radio, TV. Orthodox Jews forbid TV but allow cars. They continue their former existence in the form of a sect. Members of the sect do not have a cultural identity problem because they stick, rigidly, to their original traditional culture. The assimilationists do not have a cultural identity problem because they assimilate into Western civilisation. Assimilation can be successful as in the case of Marx, Freud, Disraeli, Einstein, Trotsky, and many others less famous. The adaptationists face the big problem: can a traditional culture be adapted and still retain the quality of the original culture, or does this adaptation introduce changes which make the new version qualitatively different from the original one?

I believe that when one tries to adapt an inherently religious culture to Western secular culture the change is qualitative. I believe all adaptationist enterprises must end in assimilation. The elements of the traditional culture the adaptationists try to retain lose the power they had in the original culture. They are like a Coat of Arms, a beloved symbol which once induced motivation and today induces only nostalgia. Adaptationist cultures share the assumptions and motivations of Western civilisation even if the garb is traditionalist. The garb expresses what they would like to be, the motivations what they are.

Can Jewish cultural identity be adapted to secular Western culture and still retain its Jewish quality? My answer is no. I am convinced this is impossible. So what about the Bund, Yiddishism, Zionism, etc. and all others who labelled themselves Jewish (and genuinely felt Jewish) despite the fact that they no longer adhered to the 613 mitsvot, and embraced modernity, that is, Western atheist culture?

The Jewish religion has two peculiarities which make it very different from Christianity or Islam:

1. It is a tribal religion. It merges religion and ethnicity into a single entity. In this religio-ethnic culture the religious component dominates the ethnic one. In other words: Jews who reject the religion find it necessary to redefine their ethnic identity. An Arab has no need to redefine himself as Arab ethnically when he ceases to be religious. Arab ethnicity does not depend on religion. Jewish ethnicity does.
2. The Jewish religion, unlike Christianity or Islam, is theocentric. One worships God not in order to gain benefits for oneself or for one's country, state, nation, but because this is the only act worth living for.

These two peculiarities of the original Jewish identity pre-empt any attempt of secularisation.

I am fully aware of the great Yiddish culture that emerged in Tsarist Russia during the nineteenth century. I have great sympathy with it and with the Bund. But they were cultural identities in their own right. They emerged from traditional Jewish identity with residues of the original culture, but they rejected most of its assumptions and expectations. If Bundists lit two candles on Friday night they did so not to the mark the start of a day dedicated to God but to mark respect for their ancestors.

The atheist Israelis differ so little from atheist Americans as to justify the term 'Hebrew-speaking Gentiles'. Atheism contradicts

Jewishness. The Zionists substituted secular nationalism for belief in God. When they finally succeeded in establishing their secular state they discovered that they were unable to provide a secular definition of Jewishness and had to accept the religious definition. They live in a permanent state of contradiction – atheists who define their ethnic identity by a religion in which they do not believe. The political success of Zionism exposed its cultural debacle.

You suggest we distinguish between Judaism as a religio-communal way of life and Jewishness as a sociological condition of Jews during the last two centures. This, however, raises three problems:

1. what are the specific features of sociological Jewishness?
2. what are the differences between Judaism and socio-Jewishness?
3. why is the label 'Jewish' valid for both cultures?

I am fully aware of what you call the 'tragedy of secular Jews', though I'd call it a 'problem' rather than a 'tragedy'. I know what it feels like to find oneself suspended between two cultural identities none of which one fully identifies with. I deeply sympathise with anyone in this situation. I have two observations which may ease the plight of people in this culturally precarious condition.

1. Turn your problem into an opportunity. Straddling two cultures gives insights into both. Mentalities with a secure cultural identity take it for granted, and lack awareness of its role and structure. Observing the breakdown of secure cultural identity provides insights into human mentality and its need for group identity. This has some similarity with a neurotic who observes the neurosis to gain insights into the nature of mentality. The insights gained can help others in similar situations. Moreover, studying the nature of one's difficulties enables one to view them from outside, thus extricating oneself from their grip.

2. Orientate yourself towards the future, not towards the past. Whatever respect one feels for one's cultural background, one ought to let bygones be bygones. The past cannot be revived, and is of little use in handling the complex problems facing us today: bio-engineering, transplants, cloning, life-support systems, test-tube fertilisation, nuclear hazards, pollution, electronic communication, space travel, etc., all these present us with problems to which traditional culture provides unsatisfactory solutions. It is imperative to create a new culture suited for the twenty-first century. This may sound utopian, even arrogant, but what else can one do when all existing cultures are found wanting? It is difficult to start anything new, especially a cultural identity, but given that existing cultural identities are found by many of their own members as lacking the ability to handle the problems facing society today, nothing else

will do. Instead of letting oneself be pulled back by the past one can try to blaze a new way to handle the present and the future.

Components of traditional cultures can be embedded in this new cultural identity, but the spirit must be one of creating a new approach rather than reshaping something old. Look at the American Indians lingering in a cultural limbo on their reservations. They cannot embrace the American culture (and I fully agree with them) but their traditional cutlure is unable to handle the modern world, and apart from folklore and nostalgia provides no clues for a meaningful existence in the modern world. The result? Alcoholism and suicides. If we wish to avoid such a state of mind we had better do something about it. Attachment to labels from the past obscures rather than assists efforts to handle modernity. In 1968 the British press didn't know how to label what they later called 'the new left' so they labelled it 'Brand X'. How about a new 'Brand X' culture?

Part Two

MYTHS

Introduction: Lies and Myths

It is a widespread habit among non-religious Jews to present themselves as victims of persecution. Some find in persecution the core of their Jewish identity, saying to themselves: I may not know exactly what my Jewishness consists of, but as long as I am discriminated against because of my Jewishness I am a Jew. All this does not apply to Orthodox religious Jews, who, despite all persecution never see themselves as victims and whose practice of the religion provides a clear, unique and positive definition of Jewish identity.

Zionism, from Herzl onwards, posited Jewish identity negatively, by relying on anti-semitism. After the establishing of Israel as an independent state in 1948 this self-image of the eternal victim was applied to Israel itself. Israel was portrayed as a state of victims and a victim state. Israelis were told by the state's leaders and by their educational system that all its wars and conflicts with the Arabs were the fault of the Arabs, who persecuted Israel simply for being Jewish. Even the flight of hundreds of thousands of Palestinians from Palestine in 1948 is presented as the Palestinians' own fault, with Israel an innocent victim of Arab propaganda. My views on this subject constitute the first essay in this part. In the second essay I offer an alternative to the official version of the Israeli–Arab conflict.

The last essay sheds light on the attitudes of Zionism to the Holocaust. Contrary to accepted opinion Zionism was not keen to rescue Jews from the Nazis. It was keen on bringing Jews to Palestine but considered efforts to help Jews reach other countries as a diversion. Ben-Gurion stressed that if the efforts of world Jewry, its money and institutions, were to be dedicated to rescuing Jews from the Nazis by helping them emigrate to countries other than Palestine then the Zionist enterprise in Palestine could become a museum piece. At the same time, he was aware that public opinion concerning the Holocaust would support the demand for a Jewish state in Palestine. In the essay on the Kastner case, light is shed on darker corners of the Holocaust. Unfortunately Kastner was assassinated before he could spill the beans about his mentors. The attitude and policy of the Zionist leadership towards the Holocaust has, so far, eluded critical appraisal. May this essay motivate further probing of the issue.

How Palestinians Became Refugees in 1948[1]

According to the British census of 1948, at the beginning of that year there were 1.1 million Palestinians living in Palestine. At the end of 1948, 700,000 of those people became refugees. The debate has raged ever since about who caused this outrage and how to rehouse, resettle, the refugees. The debate has continued inside and outside Israel.

Israeli society in 1948 was still dominated by Labour Zionism, by people who wanted to be Zionist and socialist at the same time. Ben-Gurion's party was a labour party and it was committed not only to Zionism but also to socialism. Of course whenever there was a conflict between the socialist and the Zionist conceptions the socialist conception was always sacrificed. But they had a desire to maintain a socialist stand. (And just in an aside let me say that to this very day Mr Shimon Peres is still sitting in the Socialist International. He ought to be expelled but he is still there, using it as a platform for Zionist politics.) In 1948 Labour had the majority; by no means the entire society, but a majority of 60–70 per cent, and was still committed to socialist and humanist values. These humanist values caused a debate in the ranks.

The debate was as follows. If the Palestinian refugees were really expelled by the Israeli army then they have the right to return to their homes and their villages. If they fled of their own accord then they do not have that right.

I rejected this dilemma. To my mind, even if they fled of their own accord, they have the right of refugees to return to their home. For me this was never an issue, but for the majority of Israeli society it was an issue – for all those younger people who were genuinely committed to socialism and did not realise that you cannot have socialism together with Zionism.

The Israeli government saw the necessity to create a myth, and to spread it throughout Isreali schools as well as abroad. The myth was, and I quote:

> The flight of the Palestinians from the country both before and after the establishment of the state of Israel came in response to a call by the Arab leadership to leave temporarily in order to

68

return with the victorious Arab army. They fled despite the efforts of the Jewish leadership to persuade them to stay.

As the myth was spread in the schools, the debate subsided. Then, gradually, after the war of 1967 and especially after 1977, a new kind of mentality started to emerge which grew stronger by the day, a mentality that no longer rests on socialist or humanist values. Recently a British TV journalist asked an Israeli woman for her views on the Palestinians. She replied: 'Well, they are guests in this country.' The journalist said to her: 'But madam, you came from the United States a couple of years ago. How can you say this about people who have lived in this country for 1,400 years?' She replied: 'The country belongs to us because God gave it to us, not to them, and they are guests. And therefore if they behave, fine, and if they don't behave – out.'

The next election will show which conception of the situation – the humanist or the one represented by this woman's views – will gain the majority. If the Shamir faction, the hard-line faction, gets a majority, then the old humanist conception is dead and finished. If the Shamir faction is upheld by a 30 per cent minority, and 70 per cent or 60 per cent or 55 per cent of the Israelis opt for Kahane's policies, then it is a different ball game. We are dealing with people who present a humanist façade to the outside world but who are religious fanatics – nationalistic, religious fanatics. This is contrary to the Jewish religion. According to the Jewish religion you do not worship a state and you do not worship countries, you worship God and worship of anything else is idolatry.

However, if they gain a majority in the election, then everybody should know that we are dealing with a new situation. If Peres's lot get a majority it means we are dealing with hypocrites; if Shamir's lot get a majority we are dealing with fanatics, a fanatic with 200 nuclear bombs is not a joke. It is not a joke for the Palestinians, it is not a joke for the Israelis or the Jews, and it is not a joke for the rest of the planet, because they don't give a damn – they don't give a damn about anything except themselves. They will be willing to pull down the rest of the planet if they feel threatened; make no mistake about it, everything they present to the outside world is a façade.

Immediately after the 1948 war, a debate started in Israeli society, and one of the most powerful documents in that debate was a short story of not more than 15 pages, called 'The Story of Khirbet Khiz'eh'.[2] Written in 1948 the story describes the entry of a platoon of Israeli soldiers into a Palestinian village after the war. The fighting is already over, the young people have already left the village and the Army has been ordered to expel the remaining people. One of the soldiers feels uneasy. When this story was published in Israel in 1948 it created an uproar in the country. The writer himself was a prominent member of Ben-Gurion's party; he was later a Member of Parliament and he is a very well-known writer in Israel. Though the village itself is fictional, it is a fictional version of actual events in which the writer participated.

'We reached the field next to the houses of the village, near a wide dirt track connecting the village with the road. I started to think that maybe this road had been trodden for many generations by people, and that now grass would grow here and it would grow wild and nobody would be there. Immediately I felt uneasy and there was an upwelling of rebellion within me, something which was annoying me, and I could feel how it clenched its fists, and while we were eating the oranges, Gabi, one of the soldiers, interrogated Moshe: 'What do we have to do here?'

And he said: 'It would be much better if we all leave this place and go away, let the others deal with it and, yes, we must also clean the machine gun.'

But Moshe said 'No' – he is the commander – 'first of all we have to check out all the Arabs we have collected and identify suspicious youngsters. Next, lorries will come and we will load them on to the lorries and leave the village empty. And third, we have to finish burning down the village, blowing up the houses. Then we will go home.'

We collected our equipment and we went to the centre of the village. I had doubts and I argued with myself and suddenly I plucked up the courage and said to Moshe: 'Really? Do we have to expel them? What can they still do? Who can they harm? The youngsters have already left, what is the point?'

'Ah!' said Moshe, 'but it said so on the order we received.'

'But that was wrong', I said, and I didn't know which of all the arguments within me I could best present to him as proof. And therefore I said, 'I think it is wrong.'

'So what do you want?' said Moshe, and he pulled in his shoulders and left me.

I would have preferred, too, for various reasons, to keep quiet, but since I had started I could not keep quiet and I said to my friend who was walking beside me, 'What is the need to expel them?'

'Sure,' he said. 'What do you expect to do, put the guards to guard them?'

'But how else can they harm us?'

'They can – and how! Wait till they put mines on the roads and steal from the kibbutzim and spy on everything, you will see then, see? Why not? Are they too small for you? Is there too much justice on their side? And apart from this there will always be one or two about whom you don't know anything, so what do you suggest? If you don't know then keep quiet.'

We saw then a woman passing by with a group of three or four other women. She held the hand of a child of seven. There was something special about her; she looked dignified, she looked dignified in her sorrow. Tears, which looked as if they were not her own tears, rolled down her cheeks. The child was crying, something like, 'What did you do to us?', with closed lips. It seemed as if she was the only person who knew precisely what was happening here, to such an extent that I felt ashamed and I lowered my eyes. I saw how she made an effort not to pay us any attention. We realised that she was a mother lioness. We saw the wrinkles of effort in her face to carry with dignity and with heroism her suffering, and how when all her world was lost she didn't want to break down in front of us. Elated and dignified in her pain and sorrow about our wicked existence, they passed through us, and I also saw what was happening in the heart of that child. Something was happening that meant that when this child grew up it would not be able to be anything except a hater. That child that was now crying helplessly.

And suddenly something hit me, everything suddenly sounded different, more correct. This is exile, this is exile, all this is exile, this is what exile looks like. I couldn't stand still. I rushed about to the other side where the blind people came. I rushed away from them. I went to the clearing in the cactus hedge. Something built up inside me. I was not an exile, I said to myself; I never knew what it was like and I was told in school and I read and I was told again and again in every corner, in every paper in every book everywhere, exiled! All my emotions were played on. That was an accusation our people levelled against the whole world. Exile! You exiled us. And this was inside me, probably with my mother's milk. What the hell are we doing here today? I met Moshe.

'Why are you looking at me like this?' he said.

'It is a dirty war,' I said to him.

'Please, what do you want?'

And I had something to say, only I didn't know what would be rational and not merely emotional. Somehow I had to shock him; I had to present him with the seriousness of the whole situation.

Instead, Moshe said to me, pushing his cap backwards, talking man to man, looking in his pockets for cigarettes and matches, 'Listen, what I'm telling you, immigrants will come, our immigrants, and they will take over this land and they will cultivate it and it will be wonderful here.'

Of course, why didn't I think of this myself, problems of
housing and immigration and we will bring the refugees, our
refugees, and put them here? We'll open a co-op, we'll open a
synagogue, we'll open a school. There will be parties here.
They will discuss various issues, they will cultivate the field. There
will be a new Hebrew language. Who will ever remember that
here there was once a village from which we expelled the people
and inherited the soil, where we came and we shot, we burnt,
we exploded, we destroyed, and we exiled. What the hell are
we doing in this place?

I felt that I was on slippery ground. I tried to control myself.
All my insides screamed. 'Colonizer!' screamed my insides.
'Lies,' screamed my insides. This is not ours. The machine gun
has never granted any right. 'Yes,' screamed my insides, 'what
weren't we told about refugees?' Everything for refugees, for their
welfare, for their rescue, of course, our refugees. Those that we
expelled – that's another story altogether. Wait a moment! Two
thousand years of exile and what not? Killing Jews, now we are
the masters. And those who will later live in this village, won't
the walls scream in their ears? Those sights, those unscreamed
screams, this innocence of the people we expelled from here,
the weakness of the weak that surrender, this heroism of the weak
who don't know what to do and can't do anything. Mute, weak,
won't this trouble all those who will live here afterwards?'

I wanted to do something. I knew I couldn't scream. Why
the hell am I the only one who gets upset here? What is this inside
me? There was something rebellious inside me, something
smashing everything. To whom shall I talk? They will only
laugh at me. There was a collapse inside me. There was one
idea, stuck like a nail, that it was impossible to accept this while
there were those tears in the eyes of the child, crying and going
with his dignified mother who withheld herself in order to show
nothing and went into exile carrying with her the screams of
injustice. A scream like this cannot be ignored and must be
accepted somewhere in the world sometime in the future.

And I said to Moshe, 'We have no right, Moshe, to expel them.'
And I didn't want my voice to tremble.

And Moshe said, 'You're starting again?'

And I knew that nothing would come out of him and I
became sad and I started choking. The first lorry started moving
– I didn't notice when – and it was already on the dirt track. If
I could only run from one to the other and say, 'Please, come
back, come back tonight. We are leaving this village, the village
will be empty, come back, don't leave the village empty!' But
then the second lorry moved with the women in their blue and
white scarves, and a wail came out from there and was mixed

with the wailing of the engine and the truck made its way to the West Bank.

This terrible feeling of guilt which troubled many Israelis has been papered over during the years by an intensive educational campaign perpetuating the myth – which became the dominant myth in Israel – that the Palestinian refugees ran away of their own accord. However, that myth is now being exploded, to some extent, because a lot of documents have come to the fore and because the myth is no longer necessary since Israel today has a population among whom there are many – probably the majority – who no longer need these justifications: they have God on their side, according to their understanding.

I suggest you have a look at another book because it was written by a Zionist, not by an anti-Zionist like me. He was a leading member of the Mapam Party, which wanted to be a Zionist/Marxist party, and he was the editor for many years of *New Outlook*, the monthly paper of the Mapam Party – Simha Flapan.[3] He took the myth, exploded it in about 40 pages and then came to a conclusion. The balance is clear. According to Flapan, as of 1 June 1948, by Israeli defence intelligence estimates, 370,000 Arabs left the country from both the Jewish parts and the Arab parts conquered by the Jews. Jewish attacks on Arab centres, particularly large villages, towns or cities, accounted for about 55 per cent of this number. Terrorist acts of the Irgun and Lehi accounted for 15 per cent; whispering campaigns, psychological warfare for 2 per cent; evacuation ordered by the IDF for another 2 per cent; general fear for 10 per cent. Therefore 84 per cent left in direct response to Israeli actions. Those that remained were only about 50 per cent of the entire exodus. Some were to leave the country within the next six months. So, even according to Israeli intelligence accounts, 80 per cent of those 700,000 who fled were expelled from Palestine by direct Israeli action.

Flapan's book is a left-wing Zionist critique of Israeli politics. There is no rejection of Zionism.

Another book I would strongly recommend is the one by Benny Morris, who used to be a journalist on the *Jerusalem Post*, called *The Birth of the Palestinian Refugee Problem 1947–1949*.[4] I will read a bit of the review by the *Guardian*:

> A young Israeli scholar has driven a coach and horses through the traditional Zionist explanation of the creation of the Palestine refugee problem with his discovery of a contemporary classified intelligence document assessing that 70 per cent of the first wave of the great Arab exodus in 1948 resulted from Jewish military action. The document, a secret Israeli army intelligence report dated June 30 1948 goes out of its way to point out that the

flight of the Palestinians was against the wishes of the Palestinian leaders and the neighbouring Arab states which invaded the newly-created Jewish state as it became independent.

So the myths are now being exploded, and the majority of Israelis will have to adjust to the fact that they do not have justice on their side. What will they do? They will try to mobilise God on their side, this is what is going to happen. For me the entire debate was never valid. If the Palestinians left of their own will, they also have the full right to return to their houses and to be an independent people in their own country. This was never problematic for me, but people like me are a small minority.

So I suggest that when the next Israeli election comes you watch carefully for what is happening behind the scenes and then you will get an idea whether we are dealing with a country in which humanist values still carry some weight or whether we are facing a completely new ball game – where religious bigots and nationalistic fanatics are the dominant majority.

Notes and References

1. Speech at CABU conference on 1984, London, 9 April 1988.
2. Yzhar Smilansky, 'Khirbet Khiz'eh', 1948. (Not published in English.)
3. Simha Flapan, *The Birth of Israel, Myths and Realities*, 1987, Croom Helm.
4. Benny Morris, *The Birth of the Palestinian Refugee Problem 1947–1949*, 1987, Cambridge University Press.

8

From 1948 to the Intifada: Two Versions

On 29 October 1956 Ben-Gurion ordered the Israeli Army to invade Egypt. A few hours later the French Prime Minister Guy Mollet and the British Prime Minister Anthony Eden issued an ultimatum to Israel and Egypt to stop the fighting and to retreat ten miles from either bank of the Suez Canal. As the Israeli Army was still some 50 miles from the canal the ultimatum was an invitation to Israel to continue the invasion. As the British and French Cabinets expected, President Nasser, being under attack, could not accept the ultimatum, whereupon the British and French armies, mustering for weeks beforehand in Cyprus, invaded Port Said and Suez at both ends of the canal, landed paratroopers in the canal zone, and tried to reassert Anglo-French ownership of the canal which had been nationalised a few months earlier by President Nasser.

It was quite clear that the Israeli-French-British attack on Egypt was a combined operation, planned and organised well beforehand. The Israeli attack provided the pretext for Britain and France to appear as peace-keepers whose sole concern was to keep the Suez Canal open for international shipping.

The interests of each of the aggressors were quite clear: the French and British Cabinets were furious that Egypt dared to defy their power and nationalise the Suez Canal. The economic and political implications of Nasser's nationalisation of the canal were obvious.

The French had a further interest: to topple Nasser because of his support for the FLN which was fighting for the independence of Algeria. The French believed that defeating Nasser would help them defeat the FLN. Ben-Gurion saw an opportunity to use Anglo-French hostility to Nasser for annexing the Sinai and toppling Nasser, who seemed capable of unifying the entire Mashreq from Egypt to Iraq. Ben-Gurion considered such a union to be a grave danger to Israel. This view was insufficient to convince Israelis to sacrifice their lives, therefore the official line was that Nasser was preparing an attack on Israel and that it was necessary to wage a 'Preventive War' in order to defend Israel.

Being an ex-seaman I was called up for reserve duty in the port of Haifa one week before the war started. The train from Jerusalem to Haifa passed close to the Lod airport and gave, in 1956, an unobstructed view of the main runway. I could see a squadron of French fighter planes on the tarmac. The French insignia was clear and unmistakable. The pilots, who had little to do before the war, spent their time in bars in Tel-Aviv. Dozens of French pilots in the bars of Tel-Aviv was something never seen before.

In the port of Haifa there was more unusual activity. French cargo ships anchored outside the port during daytime moved into the port at night, their names and ports of registration dubbed over with black paint, to unload French armour, tanks and mobile artillery. All this caboodle clattered – with considerable noise – through the town of Haifa in the dead of the night. Such unusual activity woke up many people puzzled by the cause of all that noise who stared out of their windows and saw the French insignia on the MX tanks. This went on night after night for a week and became the talk of that town so that even the blind heard the news. Although these events were never mentioned in the Israeli press or radio they travelled fast by word of mouth and anyone who wished could confirm the gossip by taking a bus to Lod or Haifa.

In short, it was no secret that French tanks and warplanes arrived in Israel a week before the war. Imagine my surprise when a couple of days after the start of the war, when the Soviet Union accused Israel of collusion with Britain and France, the entire Israeli public, press and most political parties exploded in a vehement, outraged denial of any connection between the Israeli attack and that of Britain and France: how dare Moscow accuse Israel, which was only defending itself against an imminent Egyptian attack, of co-operating with imperialist powers like Britain and France bent on profit and power?

The vehemenence of the Israeli Labour government was understandable. Ben-Gurion and his disciples did not want to be seen as collaborators of colonial powers like Britain and France.

The narrow-mindedness, lack of understanding of historical processes, duplicity and hypocrisy of the leaders of Labour Zionism is well known in Israel; the problem is not the leaders but the led. I was amazed to see many ordinary Israelis genuinely outraged by the Soviet accusations despite seeing the French tanks in Haifa and the planes in Lod. It was a clear case of *my mind is made up, don't confuse me with facts.*

I met many of these people and had many heated debates with them, and I can testify that although they saw the French tanks in Israel before the war they were utterly genuine in their insistence that there was no collaboration between Israel and France.

I was reminded of this schizoid state of mind when I read James Cameron's report from Jerusalem in the *Evening Standard* shortly after the 1967 war.

He concluded his article by quoting an Israeli woman whose son was killed while conquering East Jerusalem. He asked her whether it was worth it. She replied, 'The whole of Jerusalem is not worth the small finger of my son who died for it. But without Jerusalem I cannot live.' I can add another story, namely that even atheist, left-wing members of kibbutzim, who never cared about East Jerusalem, burst – to their own surprise – into hysterical sobbing when they conquered the Wailing Wall in June 1967. Something odd was going on in those minds.

It took me another eleven years to find a satisfactory answer to the question of what was happening here. It is worth noticing that the entire Zionist Labour movement, in particular Ben-Gurion and his party, but also the Marxist-Zionist MAPAM, insisted for another 30 years (from 1956 to 1986) that the Israeli attack on Egypt in 1956 had no connection whatsoever with the Anglo-French attack and was a purely defensive war that was forced upon Israel. Even the American Jewish Marxist Huberman in the American magazine *Monthly Review* insisted on this version. This vehement denial of any co-operation with Britain and France was persistently repeated by all leaders of Labour Zionism even after books by French and British politicians and generals disclosed details of Ben-Gurion's pre-war visit to France to finalise arrangements for the joint attack. As late as 1982, when Begin defended his invasion into Lebanon against criticism from the Labour benches by stating that this was not the first time Israel had attacked without being threatened, that Ben-Gurion's attack on Egypt in 1956 was the first case of an unprovoked attack to achieve political aims, the Labour opposition, headed by Mr Peres, burst into vehement denial. Every 29 October, from 1956 onwards, whenever the Suez War (known in Israel as the 'Kadesh operation') was mentioned, Labour Zionists insisted, even in mimeographed newsletters in kibbutzim, that there was no connection whatsover between Israel's war in 56, and the war of Britain and France. This went on year after year until October 1986 when for the first time Prime Minister Peres (Ben-Gurion's errand boy to France in 56) decided to celebrate publicly the thirtieth anniversary of the non-existent Franco-Israeli alliance of 56 at the Ben-Gurion University in Be'er-Sheva, and invited his French partners of old to join him. With a smile from ear to ear Peres celebrated the collusion he and his mentor Ben-Gurion had vehemently denied for 30 years. What can one say of the minds that hatched this monumental moral and political debacle?

The Suez War of 1956 is a glaring example of schizoid mentality of both leaders and led in Israel. They cling to their image of themselves as victims under all circumstances, even when they launch an attack on a weaker party.

The Israeli outrage against the charges of collusion motivated me, and my friend Moshe Machover, to write a book that will provide irrefutable proof of that collusion. The idea was to use material published only in the Israeli press in order to show that even without other sources it was possible to prove that Israel was in collusion with Britain and France. As we started to work on the book in 1957 we gradually realised that we had to provide a political analysis of 1955, 54, 53, 52, etc. How far back should we go? As far back as 1918 or even 1897? We knew of course that the conflict between the Zionist movement and the indigenous population of Palestine had begun long before 1948, but as we decided to focus on Ben-Gurion's policy in 1956 it made sense to start in 1948, when Israel became independent and he became Prime Minister.

We decided to read every Israeli newspaper from 15 May 1948 to 19 October 1956. I went to the National Library in Jerusalem every evening after work for more than a year, and read every daily newspaper that had appeared during those eight years.

Our original view was that of the Israeli Communist Party, namely, that Ben-Gurion's primary political decision was to support the USA against the USSR, and that his conflict with the Arab states was a consequence of this choice. The Arab people, dominated and exploited by imperialism, were bound to be anti-imperialist whereas Ben-Gurion chose to support imperialism. Translated into local, Israeli, terms this meant that Israel's foreign policy dictated its defence policy. But the data did not always fit this thesis. In 1948, when the USSR supported the partition resolution of the UN,[1] Ben-Gurion was very friendly towards the USSR. In 1948 Czechoslovakia supplied Israel with rifles, machine guns and aeroplanes while Britain, France and the USA imposed an arms embargo. The Czechoslovak weapons enabled Israel to win the 1948 war and remained the standard equipment of the Israeli Army for a few years. Gradually we realised that we had to change our thesis. Our data indicated that the source of the conflict between Israel and the Arab states was the conflict in Palestine arising from the Zionist immigrants from Europe who wished to establish their own nation-state in a country that was already populated by Palestinians who had their own aspirations for independence.

The conflict was about lands and independence between the new Zionist immigrants and the indigenous Palestinians. There were Jewish communities in Palestine before the Zionists arrived (the religious Jews, and the Rothschild settlers) but they never got into a political conflict with the Palestinian population because they had no aspiration for independence and did not have 'buy Jewish only' or 'employ only Jews' policies. All this was introduced by Labour Zionist immigrants from 1900 onwards.

We discovered two additional interesting facts. First, in 1948 the Israeli public, press and politicians had no shred of doubt that they were in fact at war with Britain, not with the Arab states. Britain tried to defeat the UN resolution by fostering a local war. Second, during the 1948 war Ben-Gurion, by secret arrangement with King Abdallah of Trans-Jordan, annexed half of the territory the UN partition resolution had granted the Palestinians. By this annexation Ben-Gurion and Abdallah violated the UN resolution and became embroiled in an ongoing conflict with the Palestinians. Had Israel remained in its partition resolution borders the Palestinian grievances against it could be directed only against the UN, but from the moment Israel annexed territories granted by the UN to the Palestinians it could not invoke UN authority to legitimise its territorial annexations. Israel never achieved recognition of its armistice lines as boundaries.

These two points were in stark conflict to the versions produced by Israeli propaganda from 1950 onwards. The official versions insisted that the 48 war was between Israel and the Arab world, and that the Arab states – not Israel – violated the UN resolution.

From the moment the official versions became accepted by the Israeli public (and by the world at large) the hostility of the Arab world towards Israel became inexplicable. Zionist propaganda provided its own explanation: 'There is no territorial or political cause for the Arab hatred of Israel, it is simply the age-old hatred of Jews.' President Nasser was referred to as the reincarnation of Adolf Hitler. This fitted into the Zionist view of Jewish history as an eternal struggle against the gentiles who always and everywhere try to destroy the Jews.

This prompted me to comment on the back cover of our book: 'Many will find here for the first time a detailed description of forgotten facts. The few who know the facts will be surprised to discover the extent to which official propaganda can shape not only people's views but even their memories.'

When the book came out in 1961 (entitled *Peace, Peace, and No Peace*) no one – not even the Communist Party – accepted the idea that the conflict with the Palestinians was the source of the Israel–Arab conflict. People argued that although the Palestinians had formed a coherent community until 1948 they became fragmented as a result of the 48 war into three groups – refugees, Jordanian subjects and Israeli subjects – and their cohesiveness was a thing of the past. We argued that despite this fragmentation most Palestinians did not lose their aspiration to be a free people in their country – Palestine. Today, in 1990, after three years of Intifada, few will contest this view, but in 1960 no one in Israel accepted it. Where were all Israeli academic experts on the Arab world, the Arab Affairs advisers, the political commentators? Why couldn't they see in 1961 that the Palestinians did not disappear from history? They were all, every one of them, concerned with their careers, status and income, and had no inclination to come up with an observation that might rock the Zionist boat.

Peace, Peace, and No Peace made no impact even in anti-Zionist circles. At the time I still believed that if only people knew the genuine facts they would change their minds. It took me a few more years to conclude that facts do not possess an innate significance and that people interpret them according to their own needs, and according to their anxieties.

Was it therefore a waste of time and energy to write that book? I don't think so. The handful of people who accepted the version presented in the book later formed themselves into the 'MATZPEN' group and, after the 1967 war, publicly confronted the official Israeli version of the conflict in Palestine with an alternative version. In the light of the fires lit by the Intifada there can be little doubt which version is the valid one.

It is never a waste of time to provide an alternative version to an official view that is taken for granted. Once an alternative version exists the official version can no longer be taken for granted. A new situation is created which forces those concerned about the issue to choose between two interpretations of the events.

When people have to choose they become aware of their responsibility for the consequences of their choice. Absence of choice means absence of responsibility. 'We have no choice', used to be the central justification of Israelis for their government's policies. Begin's invasion of Lebanon in 1982 was the first occasion on which many Israelis began to question this myth. Most Israelis now accept that Begin's invasion of Lebanon was a matter of choice. They have not yet accepted that they also had a choice in 1948 (not to annex the Palestinian part of Palestine) and in 1956 and 1967 (not to attack Egypt). Even in 1990, after three years of Intifada, many Israelis still insist that holding on to all the territories conquered in 1967 is a matter of necessity, not choice.

'We have no choice,' they insist, clinging to the self-image of the eternal victim, 'we are only defending ourselves'. If they accept that they had a choice then they must give up their image of themselves as eternal victims. Most of them cannot afford to do so.

Note

1. The decision to partition Palestine into two parts and create two states there, one for the Palestinian Arabs and one for the Jews. This was approved by a two-thirds majority of the General Assembly of the UN on 29 November 1947.

9

The Kastner Case, Jerusalem 1955[1]

In 1954 I was a student at the Hebrew University, Jerusalem, when the papers announced that the Israeli government was suing for libel a 71-year-old Hungarian Jew, Malkiel Greenwald, who had accused another Hungarian Jew, Dr Israel (Rudolph) Kastner, of collaborating with the Nazis in Hungary during 1944–45.

Like most other Israeli youths I was surprised and puzzled by this news. For me – and for many others – the questions raised were: who is this Greenwald, and who is this Kastner? What exactly did Greenwald say about Kastner? Where did he say it? Why didn't Kastner himself sue for libel? Why did the government find it necessary to sue an individual for libelling another individual? How was it possible for a Jewish collaborator with the Nazis to live in Israel for nine years without being publicly denounced?

Greenwald had come to Palestine in 1938 from Vienna, where he had been badly beaten up by the Nazis. Many of his family were exterminated in Auschwitz. He ran a tiny family hotel in Jerusalem, and wrote pamphlets entitled: *Letters to my Friends in the Mizrahi* (Mizrahi was a small political party of religious Jews who supported Zionism). He mailed his pamphlets to selected members. In Pamphlet 51 (mailed in 1952) he accused Dr Israel Rudolf (Rezso) Kastner, aged 48, of collaborating with the Nazis in Hungary during the period 1944–45 and of assisting them in their extermination of some 500,000 Hungarian Jews. Greenwald called for a public enquiry committee to investigate his accusations.

Kastner himself came from Kluj (now in Rumania), a town with a Jewish community of some 20,000 which was annexed by Hungary during the war and was known as Koloszvar. He was born in Kluj, and from 1925 to 1940 was the political editor of *Uj Kelet* (New East), the Jewish daily paper in that town. From December 1942 till the Soviet army entered Budapest in February 1945 he headed the Jewish Relief Committee in Budapest, which was affiliated to the Relief Committee of the Jewish Agency in Palestine (the 'Agency' was, in effect, the 'government' of the Jewish community in Palestine, and as such the spearhead of the entire Zionist movement). He arrived in Palestine in 1946 and joined Ben-Gurion's ruling party MAPAI (the Zionist Labour Party, 'Land of Israel Workers Party'). He became a MAPAI candidate to the first Knesset, was given the post of Spokesman of the Trade and Industry Ministry, was appointed Director of Broadcasts in Hungarian and Rumanian languages on the state's radio, was appointed Chief Editor of *Uj Kelet* (the same title as his old paper), MAPAI's paper in Hungarian, as well as Chairman of the Organisation of Hungarian Jewry. In other words, he was head of the Hungary department of the ruling party.

This information, from the daily press in Israel, answered some of our first questions. It was obvious that Kastner was a prominent figure of the Israeli establishment and had either to clear his name or be sacked. But why didn't Kastner himself sue Greenwald? Had Kastner sued Greenwald and lost his case he would be liable to prosecution under Israeli law for sentencing Nazis and their collaborators (1950), the only crime in Israel for which the death penalty exists. Could it be that the establishment had decided to sue because Kastner's failure to do so would have implicated others above him? His posts indicated that he had connections with the very top of the ruling party (Prime Minister Sharett noted in his *Personal Diary* on Saturday 27 February 1954: 'At 9 a.m. [a meeting with] Israel Kastner (one of the leaders of the Zionist organisation in Transilvania) testifying for some days in a libel case initiated by the Attorney General in his defence (as a state employee) ... .'[2] We don't know what was discussed in that meeting, but it emerged during the trial that Sharett was involved in the issue.

I attended some of the hearings in the tiny court room in the Russian Compound in Jerusalem and, like most Israelis, followed the press reports about the trial. A law student friend became the assistant to the defence lawyer and provided me with more details. What emerged was beyond anything I – and most Israelis – could have imagined; even the judge and the two attorneys had to repeat their questions occasionally due to disbelief. New, alarming and unexpected questions emerged that have never been answered.

The Trial

What became popularly known as the 'Kastner trial' was, legally, a trial not of Kastner but of Greenwald, who was sued for libel by the Israeli government. Kastner was a witness for the prosecution. But it was the pressure of the questions of the defence, and his own evasions, contradictions and lies that transformed Kastner from a witness into a defendant.

The Attorney General filed his libel case against Greenwald on 25 May 1953. The trial began on 1 January 1954. The case was known as Criminal Case 124/53, in the District Court, Jerusalem, the Attorney General against Malkiel Greenwald, before the President of the Court, Dr Benjamin Ha'levi.

The final hearing was on 3 October 1954. The hearings lasted about 70 days during which 52 people testified, some more than once. Kastner himself took the witness stand ten times. The prosecution provided 130 documents, the defence 180. The summing up of the defence lasted 30 hours. After the hearings Ha'levi retired for nine months to consider the case (there is no jury system in Israel, and the judge alone must decide whether a witness has lied or told the truth, and whether that truth is partial or complete). On 22 May 1955 Ha'levi began to read his judgment.

He grouped Greenwald's accusations against Kastner under four headings:

1. collaboration with the Nazis
2. 'indirect murder' or 'preparing the ground for murder' of Hungary's Jews
3. sharing plunder with a Nazi war criminal
4. saving that war criminal from punishment after the war.

After an exhaustively reasoned judgment of 200 pages, he ruled that apart from the third charge all charges were true and therefore not libellous. Charge 3 he found not fully proven, and he fined Greenwald a symbolic single Israeli pound. He ordered the government to pay the costs of the trial.

During the trial one of the witnesses, Phillip von Freudiger, the political leader of the religious (Orthodox) Jewish community in Hungary, had submitted a document stating that when the Nazis entered Hungary in March 1944:

> ... anyone known as anti-Nazi, or not completely pro-German, was arrested ... within 36 hours the public arena was cleared completely of all courageous and conscientious figures ... who could cause problems for the Germans ... the way was open for political and economic adventurers, for politicians whose whole purpose was to achieve the power they coveted and for which they would have sold their soul to the devil.[3]

Ha'levi used Freudiger's last phrase in his judgment when he stated '... by accepting this gift [the Nazi promise to allow 600 Jews selected by Kastner to travel to a neutral country] Kastner has sold his soul to the devil'.[4] The press headlines next morning were: *'Ha'levi: Kastner has sold his soul to the devil'*, and that is how the case became registered in the minds of most Israelis in 1955.

Prime Minister Sharett noted in his *Personal Diary* on the day of the verdict: 'Kastner. A nightmare, horrific, what did the judge take upon himself? The party suffocates. A pogrom!'[5]

The government immediately appealed to the Supreme Court. It took another three years before the five members of the Supreme Court gave judgment. Before that, on 3 March 1957, Kastner was shot by an Israeli and died two weeks later. I shall discuss the appeal and the assassination later.

Background to the Case

During the Second World War Hungary was a willing ally of Germany and sent troops to fight against the Russians. The Nazis did not invade the country. However, early in 1944, as it became clear that the Nazis were going to lose the war, and the Russians were already driving the German Army out of nearby Rumania, Admiral Horthy, the Head of State, tried to negotiate a separate peace treaty with the British. On 19 March 1944 the Nazis invaded Hungary to prevent any separate peace.

On that day a special SS unit whose sole purpose was the extermination of the Jews, headed by Adolph Eichmann (head of department 4B in the SS) entered Budapest.

Eichmann had only 150 SS people with him, and could muster a few thousand Hungarian soldiers. The Jewish community in Hungary numbered some 800,000. Of these, 300,000 lived in Budapest and the rest in the provinces. Most of the Jews were living among the Hungarians. Eichmann decided to deal first with the Jews in the provinces, and later with those in Budapest. His task was divided into three stages:

1. locate and mark the Jews (by the yellow star)
2. move them into special concentrated areas (ghettos)
3. deport them from the ghettos to Auschwitz.

As the German Army was busy fighting the Russians Eichmann could not rely on its help. Even to secure the necessary trains was a problem. And yet between 15 May and the end of June some 500,000 Jews from the provinces boarded the trains to Auschwitz, roughly 12,000 per train, often four trains a day, and were gassed there. When this became known in the West, Roosevelt sent a strong letter to Horthy, and bombers to bombard Budapest. The deportations were stopped for a while. The Nazis continued their efforts, and on 16 October they engineered a coup which ousted Horthy and handed power to the Arrow-Cross (Hungarian Fascists) who continued the massacre of Jews with a vengeance. The Russians entered Budapest on 16 January and saved its remaining Jews.

> The Liberation of the Jews, who had been living under the dark shadow of sudden death for so long, was exclusively the merit of the Red Army and its offensive spirit. The armies of Tolbukhin

and Malinowski occupied the capital in the nick of time. A delay of only a few days would have meant total annihilation for the Jews. Nobody could have stopped the rioting Nylias ('Arrow-Cross') horde, blood thirsty and undisciplined as it was.[6]

How Could it Happen?

Why did half a million Jews, many of whom were young and had military training in the Hungarian Army, board the trains to the gas chambers without making any effort to hide, escape or resist?

The answer, which sounds unbelievable, is simple; the Jews who boarded the trains did not know that they were heading for Auschwitz. Many knew about Auschwitz, some believed it, some didn't, but all were led to believe that the trains were transferring them to another place in Hungary for 'resettlement'. Some even made special efforts to get on the earlier trains in order to get better housing in the new settlements ...

Given the acute shortage of Nazi manpower and the general retreat of the German Army, Eichmann knew that it was absolutely essential that the destination of the trains be kept secret from the Jews. Had they known their destination they would have made every effort to avoid deportation, and many could have escaped. Eichmann knew that the Jews would not trust the Nazis or the Hungarian authorities. The only people they would trust were their own leaders. He and his staff had to make sure that the Jewish leaders would not inform the rest of the Jews about the destination of the trains. The questions Ha'levi had to answer were:

1. did the Hungarian Jews know that the trains were going to Auschwitz?
2. did the Jewish leaders know that the trains were going to Auschwitz?

Ha'levi determined, from witnesses and documents, that the majority of Hungary's Jews did not know that the 'resettlement' trains were heading for Auschwitz, whereas Kastner and other Jewish leaders did know. Moreover, when the trains arrived at Auschwitz the Nazis forced some Jews to write postcards saying 'I have arrived. Am well', postmarked 'Waldsee'.[7] These were handed to Kastner who had them distributed among those still awaiting deportation. Other postcards mentioned Kenyermeze (a fictitious Hungarian place) as their origin.[8] These facts were not challenged by the Supreme Court which discussed the appeal against Ha'levi's judgment.

To substantiate Ha'levi's conclusion a report, dated April 1944, by a Jew who had escaped from Auschwitz provided detailed information on Auschwitz plus a warning to Hungary's Jews about the preparations being made in Auschwitz for their extermination. His report became known to Jewish leaders in Czechoslovakia and Hungary before the deportations began. It also reached the West. The author of that report, Rudolf Vrba, wrote in 1966:

> Even today few can believe that 400,000 human beings collaborated by their mere passivity in their own brutal destruction. Some historians, indeed, seem puzzled by this contradiction of the well-known biological facts concerning self-preservation, despite all the proof that it happened – the trials, the silent testimony of the principal witnesses.
>
> Yet the answer to the riddle is very simple. The victims were kept in ignorance of their real fate until the last possible moment, often until they entered the gas chambers, when nothing was left to them but to die.
>
> They had been told repeatedly by the Horthy propaganda machine that they were going to resettlement areas, to ghettos, to 'reservations for Jews in the East', where they would have to 'work hard', but would be safer than they were at home, where pogroms threatened constantly.
>
> No denial came from their own leaders and so they believed it all, as Major makes clear when he writes: 'Many survivors and witnesses affirmed that they either had not heard of the extermination camps, or, if they had heard about them, did not believe it.'
>
> No doubt before they left Hungary, they were worried about the real nature of their sinister, unknown destination; but there is a difference between vague suspicion and exact knowledge. They were people who had spent their lives under civilized influences and thus they were inclined to hope in their darker hours that, by obedience, they might avoid a massacre of their children. The Jewish leaders in Hungary, though knowing the truth, the detailed facts about Auschwitz, did nothing to dispel this unrealistic hope.
>
> Had they spoken, they might have changed the history books which record mournfully that 400,000 Jews were transported to Auschwitz and died without resistance. As an ex-prisoner of Auschwitz-Birkenau, one who was forced to witness from the closest possible quarters the functioning of this annihilation apparatus, I cannot emphasize sufficiently strongly that secrecy was the main key to its successful operation.
>
> The Fascists in German-occupied or semi-occupied countries, under the protection of and with encouragement from the authorities, created a pogromistic atmosphere. Against this background, the Jews were hoodwinked into going voluntarily to the 'resettlement areas'. When they arrived and realized they

had been swindled, they were inside the confines of the extermination camps, which were, for all practical purposes, watertight. In most cases, indeed, as I have said, they were inside the actual gas chambers or at their gates. Their only choice was between being wounded and tortured to death or dying less elaborately.

Often they were killed before they had time to think, to weigh the alternatives, for that was a vital part of the mass annihilation technique. While I was in Auschwitz (June 30, 1942 to April 7, 1944), I saw this process going on daily, but on a smaller scale than that of the Hungarian holocaust. During my time there, the daily quota was 'only' 1,000 to 5,000 victims. From January 1944, however, I witnessed unusually extensive technical preparations, designed to step up the intake of this murder machine to 20,000 victims a day. It was no secret in Auschwitz that these extraordinary preparations were designed for the rapid annihilation of Hungary's Jews, who were almost 1,000,000 strong.

In March 1944, after the complete occupation of Hungary by the Germans, it was evident to us Auschwitz prisoners that the start of this well-prepared action was quite imminent.

It was equally clear that the whole complicated annihilation procedure could be slowed down by revealing the secrecy of the 'resettlement areas' to its potential victims, by exposing the extermination machinery to the world in general and the Jews in particular.

With this in mind, Fred Wetzler and I escaped from Auschwitz-Birkenau on April 7, 1944, and reached Slovakia 14 days later. We immediately contacted the Jewish leaders and, at meetings in Zilina on April 24, 25 and 26, informed them in detail of what the Nazis had in store for the Hungarian Jews. The information contained in our testimony to them (the 'Auschwitz Report') contained all technical details of the annihilation process.

The leaders of Hungarian Jewry were in full possession of these facts by the end of April, 1944, at the latest. This can be confirmed by the surviving members of the Jewish Committee in Slovakia, Dr. O. Neumann, Mr. Krasnansky and Mr. Steiner, the first two of whom now live in Israel.

The facts of our report were supported by Rabbi Michael Dov Weismandel, whose own report on Auschwitz to the Hungarian Jewish leaders incorporated that by Wetzler and myself, though he improved it, naturally, by rabbinical style and authority.

... Wetzler and I saw the preparations for the slaughter. Morgowicz and Rosin saw the slaughter itself. It was their description of it that the Rabbi quoted, proof, indeed, that Wetzler and I were not exaggerating. So the Jewish leaders knew what was happening, even when they were lending their administrative help to the Nazis by preparing lists of deportees. Those who did not know were the men, women and children who were herded on to the trains when the deportations began in the middle of May, 1944. They went on day and night. Sometimes at a rate of 10,000 or even more daily (see A. Eichmann's 'Memoirs', *Life*, January 1961).

They boarded those trains passively with or without their families. They did not know that their fate was sealed as tightly as the trucks that carried them, that death was awaiting most of them and all their children at the other end of the line. I make no apology for being repetitious because it seems that it is necessary.

Instead of information, the Jewish leaders provided the adults with sandwiches and the children with milk for the journey. Had these had knowledge of hot ovens instead of parcels of cold food, they would have been less ready to board the trains and the whole action of deportation would have been slowed down. This is accepted by the historian Gerald Reitlinger, versatile though he is in the English art of understatement (see his *The Final Solution*, NY, 1953).

On p. 427 of this well-known work, he writes: 'On April 7, two Slovak authors of the War Refugee Board Report made their sensational escape from Birkenau (the annihilation centre in Auschwitz) to Bratislava. The knowledge contained in this report could at this time have saved at least 200,000 lives.'

On page 540 of the same book, Reitlinger writes about the Auschwitz report: 'The author, who had been registrar of one of the Birkenau infirmaries, was exceptionally accurate and conveyed his report to the Swiss Red Cross as early as June, 1944, thereby making history'. But Major surely is aware of these quotations because in his article in *Jewish Currents*, Reitlinger's book is quoted liberally.

It is, unfortunately, an historical fact that, between May 15 and June 30, about 120 trains, loaded with Jewish men, women and children, left Hungary for Auschwitz, while Kastner and other Jewish leaders were negotiating with Eichmann in Budapest. They negotiated with the Nazis five years after Chamberlain, at a time when any child could have told them that they were dealing with people who understood only one brand of argument![9]

Rudolf Vrba, did not live in Israel, and was not called to give evidence in the trial. The prosecution, keen to clear Kastner, had no interest in such information, and the defence couldn't locate him. But there were many other witnesses, living in Israel, who gave similar accounts.

Levi Blum, from Kastner's hometown, Kluj, whose brother was arrested for lack of documents went to the Jewish council in Budapest to deal with the matter:

They asked me where I'm from, I said: 'From Kluj'.

They said: 'There is a good friend here, a leader dealing with the rescue'.

I said: 'Who is he?' The man said it was Mr. Kastner. I went to the Hotel to look for Kastner. There was someone there, his secretary I think, I told him my brother was arrested. He left and after I waited for twenty minutes he returned and said that Mr. Kastner was sorry but he couldn't do anything in the matter.

'What happened to your brother?'

'I do not know what happened to him.'

'When did you meet Kastner?' asked Tamir [the defence lawyer].

Blum: 'In 1948, or the beginning of 1949. I saw that there was a reception at the corner of Diezengoff Street. Dr. Arne Marton [a leader of the Hungarian community] rose to speak. He said to Kastner something like: 'You'll get a street named after you even before you get a flat'. This was too much for me. I jumped up and said: 'You are making a great mistake gentlemen,' and to Kastner I said: 'You are the only one who was the best friend of Eichmann, and you were a Quisling, you are a murderer.' I asked him to sue me because I am too poor to sue. And I added: I know that you are responsible for the Hungarian Jews, mostly from Kluj, who went to Auschwitz without knowing where they were being sent and what the Germans intended. You knew where they were being sent and what the purpose of the Germans was. Kastner did not reply. I continued and asked: 'Why did you send postcards from Kenyermeze?' Someone in the audience jumped up and said: 'That was Kohani!'. Kohani was also in the hall, he stood up and said: 'Yes, I received those postcards,' I then asked: 'From whom did you receive them?' He replied: 'It's none of your business, I don't owe you a report.'

The judge stops the witness: 'Was this in public?'

Blum: 'Yes, there were a few hundred people there.'

Tamir: 'When did you meet Kastner again?'

Blum: 'The war of independence began, I was in the army; it was before the elections to the first Knesset. I suddenly see that Kastner was a candidate to the Knesset for MAPAI [Ben-Gurion's party], it stated: "Dr. Kastner, head of the Rescue committee in Hungary". Your honour, when I read this the blood rose to my head.'

'What did you do?'
'I have a good friend' [Yambur a journalist from Al-Hamishmar]. I went to him and said: 'look Yambur bachi, Kastner again!'[10]

The Deal

Many more witnesses gave similar evidence. The facts were overwhelming and were not challenged by the prosecution. Ha'levi faced a new question: 'Why did Kastner (and other leaders of Hungary's Jews) withhold from their communities the information that the 'resettlement' trains were heading for Auschwitz? Ha'levi states in the judgment:

A few days after this letter [of 25 April 1944, from Kastner and his deputy Brand, to Sally Meyer in Switzerland, asking for $2 million to bribe the Nazis], in the last days of April, Kastner received the black news from Auschwitz (the preparing of the gas chambers for Hungary's Jews, the railways agreement, the first deportation to Auschwitz, a secret rumour about the decision for a general deportation) which brought him to the verge of despair. From all the data he concluded that the deportation was imminent and inevitable, he suddenly realized the futility of all the lengthy negotiations conducted so far. At this moment of depression and crisis, during a meeting with Krumey [Eichmann's subordinate] requested by Kastner to decide on the continuation of the 'negotiations' (para. 26), Krumey pulled out the card authorizing 600 emigration permits. It is clear that his aim was to prevent a break with Kastner by providing him with a real interest and justification for continuing his relations with the SS, and even strengthening the relations for the imminent extermination period.

The temptation was great. Kastner was given the actual possibility of rescuing, for the time being, 600 souls from the imminent holocaust, with some chance of somewhat increasing their numbers by payment or further negotiations. Not just any 600 souls, but those he considered, for any reason, most prominent and suitable for rescue. His relatives, if he so wished, his friends if he wished, members of the movement if he wanted, and the heads of Hungary's Jews, if he wanted. The extermination plan threatened not just the communities in the provinces but also the Jews of the Capital, and Kastner didn't expect the total deportation to halt, miraculously, at the gates of Budapest. Here he had an opportunity to save his mother and wife from Budapest, his brother and father-in-law from Kluj, and all his other relatives and friends. The possibility of saving the 'prominents' of the provincial towns and Budapest appealed to him also from the public aspect. The rescue of the important people in the community due to the activity of the Rescue Committee appeared to him as a personal, and Zionist, success. A success which could also justify the entire policy of his previous leadership: his initiative to negotiate with the Nazis, his usurpation of the 'political' contact with the authorities, the exhausting negotiations, the protective relationship between the authorities and the committee. He still didn't give up completely the hope of a total arrangement with the Nazis based on the 'Europe Plan' or a similar big plan. Kastner was very pessimistic about the chances of the Jews to escape by their own efforts from the Nazi extermination machinery, which had already finished off almost all of Europe's Jews, and he saw the main hope of rescue in an agreement with the Nazis. No wonder that under these circumstances he accepted, without hesitation, Krumey's gift.

But *timeo Danaos et dona ferentes* (I fear the Greeks even when they bring gifts). By accepting this present Kastner had sold his soul to the devil. The immediate outcome of his agreement with Krumey was that Kastner became dependent on the favours of the Nazis. It cannot be said that he was independent before. Already his appeal to Wisliceny on behalf of the 'illegal' rescue committee, the negotiations with the Nazi leaders, and accepting the Nazi protection for the committee made Kastner himself, and the committee, considerably dependent on the Nazi regime. But before the agreement with Krumey Kastner was free, if all was lost, to cut off his contacts with the rulers and go underground with the committee, as was done in the Warsaw ghetto and other extermination locations. After the agreement with Krumey, Kastner was tied to the Nazis in the matter of saving the 600. As long as he had any hope that the Nazis would honour the rescue agreement – and indeed, despite some bad disillusions he had to face, the agreement was, after all, honoured – Kastner was interested, for saving the 600, to maintain correct relations with the authorities. As the general agreement with Krumey became actualized and acquired a living form by choosing Kastner's candidates for rescue – including his family (more than 20 people), friends, comrades, leaders of the Zionist movement and other prominent Jews, and as the number of the souls included in the rescue agreement continued to grow, so did Kastner's interest in good relations with the Nazis grow. The success of the rescue agreement depended, until the last minute, on the Nazi goodwill, and the last minute didn't arrive until long after the end of the extermination of the Jews in the provincial towns. Throughout this period Kastner depended on, and had an interest in, the goodwill of the exterminators, in order to achieve the rescue of his candidates.

The first promise to save the 600 was given to Kastner by Krumey, but the final decision on honouring and executing it lay with Eichmann. Kastner, who visited Eichmann with Mrs. Brand, had no illusions about the role and authority of that hater of the Jews: 'We knew we were facing the head of the Jews' extermination project but that he also held the possibilities for rescue. He – and he alone – decided on life and death' (Kastner's report, p. 38).[11]

... Kastner had no reason to assume that Eichmann got involved in rescuing Jews out of humane motives. He well knew that all Eichmann's activities were directed towards one goal – the extermination of Hungary's Jews.

The fact that during the period crucial to the fate of the Jews the head of the Rescue Committee in Budapest was tied to the head of the exterminators by a joint rescue plan, interested and dependent upon his goodwill, was, without doubt, a serious weakness in the defence system of Hungary's Jews![12]

The Choice

Ha'levi continues:

On 2 May (the day of the agreement with Krumey) Kastner was at the crossroads, one way for the rescue committee was to continue the method of free rescue which was not dependent on the Nazis, in the way prepared by the committee before the Nazis invasion and strengthened by the pioneer's organizations. The main means of that rescue method so far were warnings and 'journeys'.

With the deterioration of the situation at the end of April, the accumulating evidence for a total deportation, and the Nazi efforts to soothe the Jews and hide from them the preparations for the deportation, the duty of the committee at that moment was to spread the truth, to warn the people of the Nazi lies and plans, to strengthen the escape organization by all possible means, and to prepare the masses of Jews everywhere for organized activities at the moment of need.

The Jews in the ghettos, and until early May only part of the Jews in the provinces were concentrated in ghettos and the process was continuing, were totally cut off from any sources of valid information, even the Jews not yet imprisoned in the ghettos were confused by the waves of Nazi deceptive propaganda and the false announcements concerning their future.

Kastner possessed at that moment the first news about the preparation of the gas chambers in Auschwitz for Hungary's Jews, the agreement between the railway authorities of Hungary, Slovakia, and Germany for directing 150 deportation trains to Auschwitz, the first actual deportation of 1500 Hungarian Jews to Auschwitz, and the secret information from German agents about the decision on a total deportation.

Spreading this substantive news among the leaders of the Jews, especially the Zionists, in the provincial towns, and through them to the masses, could, more than the earlier general warnings by holocaust refugees which were received with indifference and disbelief, warn the leaders and the masses about the real danger of the imminent total deportation facing Hungary's Jews, and immunize them against Nazi deceptions. Spreading the truth about the actual preparations for the deportations to Auschwitz could have undone not only the Nazi disinformation plots in the provinces or made it harder to implement them, but was also a first condition for preparing the people for any organized action like large scale escape, hiding children with [non-Jewish] Hungarians, disrupting the efforts to concentrate the Jews and the preparations for deportation, passive or active resistance to the deportation, defence or sabotage.

I do not say that all these means were suitable or possible everywhere, at every stage and in every case, but that only when faced with the alternative of Auschwitz would the Jews, leaders as well as the people, have been able to consider fully and properly the ways and means suitable for defence or rescue according to the circumstances of the place and the time. There is no doubt that this way – the free rescue method independent of the Nazis – was dangerous to all involved in it and its results were not guaranteed in advance. It was impossible to know how many would be rescued in this way and it was impossible to take it unless it was done without their knowledge and against their will.

The other way opened for Kastner by Krumey was the method of rescuing Jews by the Nazis themselves, with their help, according to agreement with the SS. This way was convenient and offered predictable results. The number of Jews saved in this way was fixed, and it was possible to determine in advance who would be rescued. True, the number of candidates for rescue by this method was very small, but, as stated, it could be increased by further negotiations and large ransom payments.

The head of the Rescue Committee had to decide and choose between these two ways. It was difficult to vacillate for long and hold the rope at both ends: to enjoy Nazi help to rescue the 'Prominents' and also to save ordinary Jews by anti-Nazi methods. Perhaps the desire to attract the Committee made the Nazis close their eyes to smaller rescue efforts like forging of documents, financing 'journeys' on a small scale. But it was clear that the Nazis could not allow Kastner to warn the Jews in the province towns about their lies and plots, or to organize them to disturb the deportation plan. The totalitarian authority forced Kastner – like anyone seeking its benefit – to face a sharp choice: with us or against us. The moment he chose one way he gave up the other.

To take both ways together Kastner would have had to deceive the Gestapo and the 'Juden-Commando', an extremely difficult and dangerous task. It was not without reason that Eichmann said to him (on another matter – Brand's mission), that he (Eichmann) was cleverer than his rivals and could not be deceived, more than once did he hint to Kastner very politely about the possibility of sending him to Auschwitz: 'Your nerves are too tense Kastner, I shall send you to Theresienstadt for recuperation, or do you prefer Auschwitz' (Kastner's report, p. 43) [Ha'levi does not give full reference].

Indeed, one of the main reasons that Kastner and the members of the Rescue Committee were not sent to Auschwitz, despite their connections with the Pioneers underground, was that Kastner chose the second way: dependence on the Nazis goodwill and preferred it to the first method. Eichmann was interested to prevent the Jewish and Zionist rescue and defence system from developing in an anti-Nazi direction.

Kastner did not dare to deceive the Nazis by double dealing. From the moment he chose the joint rescue method with the Nazis (rescuing the prominents) he remained loyal to his method and to his partners in this rescue. Not merely the threat of Auschwitz prevented him from any serious deviation from this line. Kastner knew that any anti-Nazi act on his behalf or of one of his subordinates would endanger and foil the rescue of the prominents, a rescue operation he began and whose success was dependent on Nazi goodwill. Kastner didn't want to destroy with his left hand what he built with his right. He also didn't want to endanger the lives of those who relied on his rescue. For these reasons Kastner had to walk the line for rescue determined for him by the Nazis.

The rescue agreement with the Nazis forced Kastner and the Committee to give up any rescue operation which would endanger this agreement. Kastner and the Committee had to give up the independent rescue method; they had to refrain from a real warning of the Jews in the provinces, from organizing large scale escape, not to mention organizing resistance or disturbing the deportations. They had to stop or refrain from efforts to save the public or part of it by any suitable means, and had to restrict and confine the activity of the Committee to rescue specific people previously agreed to by agreement with the Nazis.

The real meaning of the rescue agreement between Kastner and the SS was to make the rescue which depended on the Nazis – the rescue 'authorized' by the rulers – the only rescue method of the committee. Giving up the free rescue was the price paid by Kastner for the rescue 'authorized' by the SS.[13]

... An admission by Kastner that he put the fate of all rescue on the Nazi card alone is implied in that part of his report where Kastner describes his deliberations on 3 June due to Eichmann's temporary refusal to honour his word about the rescue of the prominents in Kluj and the provincial towns (para. 39).

In that part says Kastner:

It was clear to me what is now in the balance. It is not a matter of saving a few hundred Jews from the provinces. If here and now Eichmann can't be made to compromise, then the committee, which in roulette played with human lives bet on the German number, would be a no less naive loser than so many others before us in conquered Europe. Then the millions paid would not only have been a folly. The loser in that game would also be called a traitor.[14]

A Double Secret

The agreement with the Nazis to keep the real purpose of the ghettoisation process and the real destination of the deportation trains secret implied that the mere fact that there was an agreement also had to be kept secret. Ha'levi commented in his judgment:

The agreement with the SS imposed on Kastner the duty of secrecy. It was a 'Reich secret'. Already at the early stages of the negotiations at the stage prior to the agreement, Kastner was warned by Krumey that the plan for the emigration of the 600 and everything related to the negotiations constitutes a 'Reich secret', and only with difficulty did Kastner inform Kraus [the Jewish Agency representative in Budapest], who was responsible for 600 immigration permits to Palestine, of the secret of the 'aliyah camouflaged as deportation' (para. 23).

The heads of the SS forbade Kastner at the beginning of the negotiations to have any contact with the Hungarian authorities. They insisted on the secrecy of the negotiations. On 10 May Kastner was arrested by the Gestapo and during his two day detention was interrogated by Klages, Head of the Gestapo, about his connections with Grezoli, member of the Hungarian General

Staff, and about information on the negotiations with the SS which he divulged to Hungarian circles. (Kastner's report, p. 34)

Rescuing the prominents of the provincial towns was a 'Reich secret' kept both from the Hungarians and from the Jews of the provincial towns.[15]

... Why was it forbidden to reveal to inhabitants of Kluj, and even – according to Kastner – to most of the rescued themselves until they left Kluj, the 'rescue secret'?

The truth is that both Eichmann and Kastner had an interest in keeping the rescue plan secret. Eichmann's words to Kastner on the danger of murders in the ghetto hint at this common interest. Had the ghetto inmates known or worried that the Nazis intended to send them to Auschwitz and the prominents to safety there could have been a rebellion endangering the prominents and the deportation plan as well. Not only a clear and complete knowledge of the Nazi plan to destroy the majority and rescue the minority but any partial information, any escape detail on an early agreement between Kastner and the SS for a separate rescue of the prominents could raise suspicions among Jews. The success of the extermination plan depended on surprising the Jews and on totally misleading them; to this end it was necessary to remove suspicions from the victims. To ensure the success of his task Eichmann imposed a total blackout on all his plans, including the plan to rescue the prominents. The sheer term 'rescue' could hint to the victims about the danger of extermination, therefore it was preferable to the heads of the SS that Kastner talked of aliyah [immigration to Palestine].

Dr. Hermann, one of the Zionist leaders in Kluj, and of the heads of the Bergen-Belsen transport [a Nazi concentration camp in Germany where the 'prominents' stayed for a while] testified (pp. 380, 382):

> In our eyes it was not a train of rescue, but of aliyah, therefore we wanted to join it, to emigrate to Palestine via Spain. The possibility of aliyah in those days was of course most attractive given the cruel conditions in which we lived ... the decision then was not whether to rescue 380 out of 18000, but whether to bring about aliyah, since there was no awareness of extermination, there was an awareness of danger not an awareness of extermination.

... Kastner understood very well – and the sections above on the danger of 'murder in the Ghetto', avoiding 'attention' and maintaining the 'rescue secret' indicate that even Eichmann and his aides clarified to him fairly explicitly – that the prominents as a whole and his friends in Kluj in particular would not be rescued from the holocaust prepared for the people.

Kastner knew that the more blurred the difference between the fate of the prominents and the fate of the people the better the prospects for the success of the operation, whereas the more true information about the Nazi plans whether about the extermination of the majority or the rescue of the minority that infiltrated the ghetto the smaller the chances of the prominents to be rescued. Eichmann and Kastner were both interested, for different reasons, in keeping the 'Reich's secret'. Eichmann – for ensuring the success of the extermination, and Kastner – for ensuring the success of the rescue plan. This is not confined to the 'rescue secret' alone; the secret which Kastner describes by this innocent name, when saying 'the rescue secret had to be kept' – was in reality nothing else than a branch of that terrible central secret on which a Nazi blackout was imposed – the secret of the extermination.

The domains of rescue and extermination fed each other. Anyone divulging the 'rescue secret' revealed an inkling of the extermination secret. The prominent's rescue operation was declared a 'Reich secret' to defend and guard strictly the secrecy of the extermination plans. If Kastner was forbidden to reveal the 'rescue secret' he certainly couldn't reveal the extermination secret. If revealing the 'rescue secret' could have led to 'murders in the ghetto', revealing the extermination secret even more so. If revealing the 'rescue secret' could have sparked off disturbances and rebellion in the ghettos, could have endangered the rescue of the prominents and disrupt the total deportation, then revealing the extermination secret could have acted like dynamite, destroying all plans together. Kastner knew that any leak of the extermination secret would endanger him and the entire rescue committee and put an end to all joint rescue plans.

The association with the heads of the SS on which Kastner placed the entire fate of the rescue forced him to withhold his information about the extermination plans from the majority of Hungary's Jews.[16]

The Paratroopers

In the course of the trial the prosecution (the Attorney General) brought up a totally unknown issue, one which wasn't mentioned in Greenwald's pamphlet. His intention was to show that Kastner was trusted by the Jewish Agency.

The issue concerned the sending of three young Jews from Palestine to Hungary in April 1944 to warn Hungarian Jewry about the impending extermination, and to initiate and organise resistance or escape. The three, who had migrated to Palestine from Hungary before the war, knew Hungary well. One of them (Joel Nusbacher 'Palgi') came from Kastner's home town, Kluj, and was a member of the Zionist youth organisation headed by Kastner before the war. Another, Hannah Senesh, was the daughter of Bela Senesh, a writer and critic who was a close friend of Otto Komolly, head of Hungary's Zionists.

The three were trained by the British Army, commissioned as officers, and given the additional task of helping Allied prisoners of war and radioing military useful information to the Allies. An RAF plane dropped them into a part of Yugoslavia held by Tito's partisans, and from there they crossed the border to Hungary. They were given Kastner's address as a reliable contact.

Senesh was caught crossing the order into Hungary and was arrested. She was imprisoned in Budapest, tortured, and finally shot in October. Nusbacher arrived at Kastner's place, and as a result of their conversation decided to hand himself over to the Gestapo. Before that he managed to locate the last of the three, Goldstein, who was hiding in Budapest, and persuade him, too, to hand himself in. Both were sent to Auschwitz but Nusbacher managed to escape, returned to Palestine, and eventually became a director of El-Al, the national airline. Goldstein perished in Auschwitz.

During Kastner's cross-examination in the trial it turned out that he had attempted to hide from the court the fact that he had informed the Gestapo about Goldstein and Nusbacher while they were still free, two days before they actually handed themselves in. He asked for, and was granted, a further testimony to clarify the issue. Ha'levi states:

> The reception given by Kastner to the two paratroopers was not very encouraging. Kastner was horrified and very perturbed by their unexpected arrival (Palgi's testimony, 399; exhibit 35, 110; exhibit 40, 416). He turned pale when he recognized Palgi who entered first. His first words were: 'Are you crazy? How did you get here?' After a brief conversation with the two youths he invited them to a meeting next morning while it was still dark. During their first night the two Haganah emissaries had to stay in Nazi Budapest in a hotel watched by the police. To reduce the risk Palgi registered only one guest in the hotel book and Goldstein entered Palgi's room without registering. For some reason Kastner, despite his close links with the Pioneers' underground, was unable to find a refuge for the two paratroopers (Palgi's testimony, B.77, 426/7; exhibit 40, 416/7; exhibit 35, 110).[17]

After 20 pages of detailed analysis Ha'levi concludes:

We'll sum up the main facts as proved indisputably by the evidence mentioned so far: it has been proved that Kastner forced the two paratroopers, with extremely heavy moral pressure exercised secretly and on the basis of false explanations, to give up their duty. That Kastner informed the head of the Gestapo about the two paratroopers. That Kastner tried, by his pressure and tricks already mentioned to make the paratroopers hand themselves over to the Gestapo and succeeded at that stage with Palgi. It had also been proved that these acts were not done on behalf of the paratroopers, but, on the contrary, endangered their lives.

... the real explanation for these acts of Kastner stems from his relations with the Nazi regime. Kastner had put, as he admits (end of para. 40), all his rescue operation on the Nazi card. All his enterprise until the arrival of the paratroopers was actually on the rescue, with the help of the SS, of 700 prominents out of half a million Jews from the provinces sent to Auschwitz.

Even those didn't reach a safe shore, but only Budapest, where they were joined by 500 of capital's prominents and wealthy, and all the 1200 rescue candidates – including more than 20 of Kastner's family (his wife, mother, brother, father in law, and more) and many of his friends and comrades – waited in the SS camp for the prominents in Columbus Street, desperately awaiting the departure of the promised train to Spain. All of Kastner's hopes for the departure of the train depended on Eichmann who could have tormented him again at the last minute, as he did on 3 June (para. 39), and on Klages, head of the Gestapo, who, on 3 June intervened on behalf of Kastner and who was also in these days before the train's departure in close contact with him (testimony of Kastner and Mrs. Brand) ... Kastner gave up long ago any possible position compatible with the arrival of the paratroopers and their mission. Any Jewish resistance, particularly Zionist, among Budapest's Jews would have endangered immediately the chances of success of his efforts – the rescue of the Bergen-Belsen train – and endanger all his links with the Germans. Moreover, the arrival of the para-troopers involved Kastner in a complication touching the roots of his loyalties. On the one hand he was asked to provide shelter and assistance to two members of the Haganah who relied on his loyalty as self-evident. On the other hand Kastner had long ago given his loyalty to the Nazi regime, not out of love of the Nazis, but due to circumstances, as a pre-condition and foundation of his entire joint effort with the Nazis which depended on their goodwill. Eichmann and Klages could, and did, rely on Kastner because all the assurances and guarantees were in their hands. His most vital interests: the rescue operation, the fate of the rescued, the fate of his relatives, his own fate and safety, forced on Kastner loyalty to the ruler. The totalitarian regime did not accept 'dual loyalty' ... It was impossible to enjoy daily the favours of the ruling tyrant without reciprocating. Kastner, who knew the Nazi murderous regime from close quarters, could not deviate even minutely from this loyalty. Secret contact with paratroopers of the enemy, or knowledge of their arrival without informing the Gestapo would have constituted a serious breach of his loyalty to the Nazi regime. The vital interest of Kastner to exist and act under the protection of the Nazi regime forced him to inform Klages as early as possible of the para-troopers' arrival.[18]

As for Senesh, who is revered as a hero in Israel, Ha'levi concluded:

Apart from the futile proposal of 14 October [months after their arrest, when he asked the Red Cross and Hungarian Defence Ministry to release the three] Kastner did nothing for Hannah Senesh. Despite the comfortable possibilities of help that existed during the prolonged relaxation period [at the end of August Hungary expelled Eichmann and stopped all actions against the Jews due to pressures by the Allies, this lasted until mid-October when the Nazis and the Hungarian Fascists (the Arrow Cross) staged a coup and took over] Kastner didn't visit Hannah in prison, didn't appoint a lawyer, didn't approach the department for POWs at the Swiss Embassy, and prevented Kraus from approaching it, didn't reply to Hannah's appeals to him, didn't send her any parcel, didn't receive her mother who tried, unsuc-cessfully, to see him, didn't inform the head of the committee, the late Dr. Komoly who was a family friend of the Seneshes and knew Hannah personally, about her being in prison in Budapest. Kastner admitted only a few of these facts and denied most in his testimony, but all were proved true by the reliable testimony of Mrs. Catherin Senesh [Hannah's mother] and other testimonies.[19]

Sharing the Plunder

The Black Book on the martyrdom of Hungarian Jewry by Eugene Levai states:

Grievous charges were brought against Kastner & Co. in general (Brand having left, his place was taken by his wife) because no account had ever been rendered by them in respect of the huge sums collected by that time. Similarly, Kastner never accounted for the amounts paid into his account from foreign sources. Dr. Kastner and his companions have therefore only themselves to blame if Jewish circles in general distrusted their activities from the beginning and, even up to the present time, are suspicious of their management of the funds.[20]

Ha'levi states:

Kastner contradicted himself seriously about the 'Becher Treasure'. In his letter to the Jewish Agency of 21.10.45 (exhibit 142) he informed the Executive of the Agency 'with special delight and satisfaction' based on the accompanied report by Dr. Schweiger about the treasure handed him by Becher that 'the valuables handed by the committee in Budapest were never used by the Germans, meaning they were never used in the German war effort'.

... clearly, Becher handed Dr. Schweiger only a very small part' of the property received from the committee. By contrast, Becher in an affidavit given after his release [from Nazi war criminals' prison] in 1948, stated (exhibit 74) that he gave Schweiger 'the diamonds, gold, etc. given to me by Dr. Kastner, worth some SF 2M', and Kastner, in his letter to the late Minister of Treasury, Mr. Kaplan (exhibit 22) supported Becher's claim, and gave details of the items that disappeared according to Becher and accused of negligence 'those emissaries of the Agency whose duty it was at first to guard scrupulously the fate of the suitcase ...' Kastner's version corresponds to Becher's words to Schweiger (exhibit 142) and to Becher's affidavit (exhibit 74) but is implausible and merely forms part of his continuous efforts to 'purify' Becher in the eyes of the Jewish Agency – efforts which began before the end of the war and continued afterwards.

Continuous steps to clear Becher were the joint alibi actions, the agreement to hand the treasure to the Jewish Agency, the letter of 21.10.45 (exhibit 142), and the whole of Kastner's report handed to members of the Zionist Congress. Kastner gradually prepared the ground for the decisive step – his intervention in Nuremberg on behalf of Becher in the name of the Jewish Agency. His continuous support – before Arian's report and after it – for Becher's claims about returning the plundered Jewish property is merely a part of the purification process.

... Kastner's contradictions concerning 'Becher's Treasure' do not prove that he shared the plunder with Becher. It has not been proved that he spent 'an empty and licentious' time in Switzerland, as the accused [Greenwald] stated in his pamphlet, nor has it been proved that he had considerable property after the war; on the contrary, it seems that he lived a normal life of an official living on his salary.[21]

Ha'levi held the accusation of 'sharing the plunder with a Nazi war criminal' to be unproved.

Saving Nazi War Criminals After the War

As already mentioned by Ha'levi, Kastner went to the International War Crimes Tribunal after the war (in 1945 and 1947) and gave evidence on behalf of Becher. That evidence saved Becher from the death penalty, the fate of many high-ranking SS officers. The SS itself was declared a 'criminal organisation', so that by definition all its high ranking officers were war criminals.

During the trial Kastner at first denied that he had given evidence on behalf of Nazis, but when the defence pressed him he admitted that he had testified before the German deNazification authorities (who had no authority to issue death penalties). The Attorney General Haim Cohaen, trying to help Kastner out of the contradictions in his statements, questioned him:

> 'Before appearing as a witness in the court did you consider the problem of whether it is a national crime or national sin to testify on behalf of Becher?'
> 'I certainly did.'
> 'We heard that you talked to many people and tried to convince them. But after the event did you talk to people, did you defend yourself?'
> 'No.'
> 'Did anyone tell you that you committed a national crime by testifying on behalf of Becher? Did they tell you in the [Jewish] Agency that you committed a national crime?'
> 'No.'
> 'Did you ever present this distinction between intervention and testimony before your interrogation in this court?'
> 'No.'
> 'You said that intervention is a crime whereas testimony is not. Do you know this distinction today?'
> 'I wish to answer that question with a few sentences. In the cross-examination, which proceeded as it did, I didn't always express myself in the best manner. On Becher I was asked today whether I ever stated in court that I didn't give a statement. I remember that I said I gave a statement before a member of the international court. I regret some of the statements I made regarding Becher in the cross-examination.
> '... I also don't think I formulated my testimony in this matter in the most proper form, but my testimony to the police, and to some extent my letter to the late Kaplan [Minister of Finance] indicate that I've never tried to hide my activity in this matter,

and I acted with a calm conscience and good faith in this matter. If under the pressure of a demagogic interrogation I said here and there things that I regret today it does not change my basic position on this matter.'

Cohen: 'Let us return to that statement. If you had to make that statement [on behalf of Becher] today, would you make it or not?'

'Yes, but without the last phrase. That is, I wouldn't have given it also on behalf of the Jewish Agency.'

'Would you do it in your name?'

'Yes, or I would have asked for written authorization, or showed my statement in advance.'

'But apart from that would you give that statement with the same formulation?'

'The same formulation.'

'Do you donsider this your duty as you were in that situation with Becher, or was this the duty of every decent person?'

'Every decent person should have done as I did.'

'Did you testify on behalf of any other Nazi officer apart from Becher?'

'I did not give a testimony that could help them.'

'I hear you testified against Nazis.'

'Tens of times.'

'But do you know of a case apart from Becher's [where a Jew testified on behalf of a Nazi]?'

'There was a committee of Orthodox Rabbis in USA and Canada, who, as far as I know, intervened on behalf of Shelenberg who was a war criminal.'

'How do you know they intervened on behalf of Shelenberg?'

'I saw the letter they wrote to the international court in Nurenberg, where there was also a trial of Shelenberg, and I was about to prove he was a criminal.'

'Did you appear against him?'

'Yes.'

[Haim Cohen takes out of his file a bunch of papers.]

'Did you ever see these statements? These are sworn affidavits from the Becher file in the German denazification court.'

'I don't know if this is all, but I saw them.'

'When did you see them?'

'When I was in Nurenberg the second time.'

'Did you see them before your statement?'

'No. After my statement. Part 1 I knew before but as a file I saw them when I was there the second time.'

[As the Attorney General begins to hand statement after statement to the judge he comes across a document that surprises him.]

'Your honour, I'm afraid that I've misled the court ... I have here the original English version of the affidavit ... '[22]

Kastner's affidavit on behalf of Becher before the international war crimes tribunal, whose existence was first denied by Kastner, and whose Hebrew translation was later contested by him and which the Attorney General pretended to know nothing about was suddenly found in his file, turned up by accident. It ends with the words:

> Having been in personal contact with Becher, from June 1944 until the middle of April 1945, I should like to emphasize, on the basis of personal observations, that Becher did everything within the realm of his possibilities and position to save innocent human lives from the blind fury of killing of the Nazi leaders. Therefore, even if the form and basis of our negotiations may be highly objectionable, I did not doubt for one moment the good intentions of Kurt Becher and in my opinion he is deserving, when his case is judged by Allied or German authorities, of the fullest possible consideration. I make this statement not only in my name, but also on behalf of the Jewish Agency and the Jewish World Congress.[23]

This statement was given by Kastner to the International War Crimes Tribunal, 11 August 1947. In December 1947 Kurt Becher was released by the international court in Nurenberg, which ruled that he should not be tried; he was then handed to a German deNazification court, which released him in 1948.

In a letter of 16 July 1948 to Mr Eliezer Kaplan, the then Minister of Finance, Kastner wrote: 'It is known that Becher was a former SS Colonel and served as a liaison officer between me and Himmler during the rescue operations. He has been released in the meantime by the occupation authorities due to my personal intervention.'[24]

Ha'levi states:

> Kastner knew well that Becher did not stand up 'courageously' against the current as he stated but obeyed Himmler's orders, from the Bergen-Belsen transport [the train of the 'prominents'] to the transfer of the Bergen-Belsen camp to the British, and that the initiative to all these acts was Himmler's and not Becher's. He also knew that the aim of Himmler and Becher was not to save Jews but to achieve Nazi interests – whether for the Nazi regime as a whole or for the relevant war criminals.
>
> There is no truth and no innocence in his statement 'I did not doubt for one moment the good intentions of Kurt Becher.' That statement by Kastner was a deliberate lie given on behalf of a war criminal in order to save him from being tried and

punished in Nurenberg. The defendant [Greenwald] has proved the truth of his accusation.[25]

... Kastner's behaviour, defending Becher after the war, attempting to purify him in the eyes of the Jewish Agency, and even saving him from trial and punishment as a war criminal in Nurenberg do require strong and most unusual motives but there is no need to look for the explanation in the financial domain as the accused assumed in his pamphlet. There are many signs in Kastner's report that strong personal sympathies were formed with the time between him and Becher, which blurred the natural separation between the Jew and the SS man. The prolonged collaboration of Kastner with the Nazis had its effect of blurring his sight, and the identification with his period of greatness continued to affect him after the change of period. Kastner needed the purification of Becher and his justification for justifying himself. Such, or similar motivations can explain Kastner's behaviour. But there is no need to ascertain the motive when the act has been proved.[26]

But the story does not end there. In 1960, six years after the trial, Joel Brand, Kastner's closest friend and deputy in Budapest (until he left for Palestine with Eichmann's offer to trade Jews for goods, when his wife replaced him), published a book (in Israel) in which he states:

When I investigated the Kastner affair, I searched and found Dr. Robert M.V. Kempner, the American prosecutor in those days, who later worked in Frankfurt as lawyer for Jewish compensation claims. He answered my questions:

Yes, I invited Kastner from Tel-Aviv to Nurenberg as a witness for the prosecution. Immediately after his arrival I regretted this invitation. Apart from the fact that he turned out to be a very expensive witness, and the expenses incurred by his visit were extremely high, a curious situation developed. We were, after all, the authorities of the prosecution. I consider it my duty to state explicitly that Kastner roamed the Nazi prison camp for Nazi Officers searching for those he could help by testimony or intervention on their behalf. In the end we were very glad when he left Nurenberg.[27]

Brand continues:

On 13 September 1945 [four months after Germany's surrender] Kastner stated before the Chief American Military Attorney Warren F. Farr, as follows:

According to Krumey's statement ... given in February or March 1945, Eichmann convened in Berlin, in spring 1942,

a meeting of the officers of the 4th dept. [in charge of exterminating the Jews] informing them that the German
government has decided on the extermination of Europe's
Jews, to be carried out secretly, in gas chambers ... Krumey
insisted that this secret be carefully guarded – not be revealed
by Eichmann, only a few officers of the 4th dept. knew the
details ... the entire German Reich machinery collaborated
with the 4th dept. in this task ... The officers of this dept.
moved from country to country ... the operative plan was
identical in almost all countries ... Krumey and ... were at
the head of the operations in Hungary, Austria, and Poland ...

And yet, despite this decisive testimony against Krumey, Dr.
Kastner stated before the deputy director of testimonials office
in the headquarters for rounding up war criminals, on 5 May
1948:

I first met Hermann Krumey in April 1944 ... in those days
he was an SS colonel, member of the staff for special actions
[the Nazi term for exterminating the Jews] under the command
of SS colonel Eichmann in charge of the final solution [Nazi
euphemism for 'murder'] of the Jewish question in Hungary.
As a result of my negotiations 15,000 Jews – out of 50,000
already deported [to Auschwitz] – were sent to Austria rather
than to Auschwitz. This meant that people who could work
were given jobs and their families – children, babies, old and
sick – were also not sent to the gas chambers as happened to
those deported to Auschwitz. They were saved from death.
Hermann Krumey was appointed head of a small staff placed
in Vienna as the officer responsible for that special group of
15,000 people.
   I wish to stress that Krumey carried out his duty with
commendable goodwill towards those who depended,
decisively, on the manner in which he interpreted his order.
As I spent the last three months of the war in Vienna I could
observe the facts stated here with my own eyes. I presented
Krumey with a series of proposals designed to improve the
hard conditions of people in this group and always found him
understanding and willing to help.[28]

Brand concludes:

'When I read Kastner's statement I was confused. Nobody
knew better than Kastner that Krumey was the immediate
deputy of the mass murderer Eichmann. Nobody knew better
than him that the anti-Jewish regulations pasted on houses in
Budapest, and the orders for concentrations and deportations
of Hungary's Jews were signed by Krumey.

He certainly remembered how Krumey faked innocence, stating that those who were already dead in Auschwitz were transferred from Hungary to 'Waldsee' in Germany for forced labour, and even exclaimed in surprise: 'Haven't you received letters from them? You'll soon get them.' But Obersturmbahnfuhrer Hermann Krumey arrived in Hungary already crowned by glorious achievements. He was the commander in Poland of the SS deportation battalions. His pet occupation was the confiscation of Polish and Ukranian peasants' lands, the deportation of the peasants to Germany as forced labour, and the transfer of the lands to influential persons in the SS.

He it was who received for 'special treatment' the 86 children of Lidice [a Czech village whose entire population was murdered as retribution for the assassination of Heydrich], and no one has seen them since.

Hermann Krumey didn't like the front, and service in the Jewish dept. suited him admirably. This dept. didn't hold the promise of fast promotion but it gave him more power than that of generals. I cannot understand how Rezso Kastner could give such a positive testimony on behalf of this war criminal. Yet Rezso told me 'I never testified on behalf of Krumey. I never defended members of Eichmann's staff, since these were nothing but murderers of the worst kind. It was different with people like Becher.'[29]

Even as late as 17 February 1957 Kastner wrote a letter to Brand insisting:

I cannot remember that I ever testified on behalf of Krumey. When asked to confirm what, to my mind, he did for us, I presumably didn't refuse.

In my statement in London I presented Krumey as a war criminal. I described in my report how he very cynically misled me during our negotiations.

... In repeated memorandums to General Taylor I demanded a trial about the Holocaust, and when Eichmann disappeared without a trace I demanded that Krumey stand trial as the main culprit.

Brand comments 'This letter left a bitter taste in my mouth. Kastner has always denied that he gave a testimony on behalf of Krumey. Even in this letter he argues that he cannot remember having said anything. But such testimonies are not forgotten easily.[30]

Kastner's testimony on behalf of Krumey was never mentioned in the trial in 1954.

The Appeal

Following Ha'levi's verdict the government appealed to the Supreme Court. This consists of five judges each of whom reconsiders the entire case and may deliver a separate judgment. The court's verdict consists of the majority's view. All five judges agreed that the charge of sharing the plunder with a Nazi war criminal had not been proved, and hence constituted libel. As for collaboration, four judges disagreed with Ha'levi and one agreed with him, whereas on the point of 'preparing the ground for murder' all five disagreed with him. The arguments for the disagreements differed. Justice Goitein argued:

> and yet, my opinion is that we should uphold the appeal, the reason being that the libel in the pamphlet which is the subject of the trial constitutes one whole and cannot be divided and split into parts except for the convenience of analysis. If the defendant justified it in its entirety he is innocent, if he justified it only partially he is guilty of the entire charge.[31]

Justice Olshan, the president of the court, had a similar view:

> When a defendant in a libel case argues that he spoke the truth – he must, according to the law, prove the truth of all the allegations, if he did not do so he has failed in his defence. With all due respect I think that splitting the main charge into two is artificial and unrealistic.[32]

Justice Silberg argued:

> The claim of the Attorney General shrinks to one point only, namely: the subjective aspect. Kastner was convinced and believed that there is no shred of hope for Hungary's Jews: not even for one, and if he, as a result of this absolute despair, didn't reveal the secret of the extermination in order not to undo or endanger the rescue of the few, then he acted innocently and cannot be charged with collaboration with the Nazis in facilitating the extermination of the Jews, even if he, de facto, contributed to this result.
>
> I must say that I cannot accept this argument. Is this 'innocence'? Is there 'representation' of despair? Can a single individual, even jointly with some friends, despair on behalf – and without the knowledge – of 800,000 people? Let us consider – and that is the crux of the matter in my opinion – the charges of the witnesses against Kastner is not that but for the guarding of the 'extermination secret' a large part of the Ghetto inmates could have been saved by one major rescue operation, organized, on a national scale; this is not the argument. The argument is that had they known about Auschwitz, thousands, or tens of

thousands could have managed to save their lives by partial, sporadic, or many individual rescue acts, like: local uprisings, resistances, escapes, hiding, hiding children with Gentiles, forging documents, paying ransom, bribes, etc. And if so, and since we speak not about a few seeking rescue, nor about a few thousands, but of many thousands, how dare an ordinary mortal reject, with total certainty, and decide with an absolute 'No' the efficiency of all this multitude and variety of rescue possibilities? How can he test those tens of thousands possibilities? Is he a god?

Indeed, he who behaves with such usurpation towards the last hope of hundreds of thousands cannot claim the defence of innocence. The burning question of 'by what authority?' and 'quo warranto' is an adequate answer to such a claim of bona fide.[33]

And yet Justice Silberg argued that whereas the charge of collaboration was fully proven, the charge of 'preparing the grounds for murder' was not, arguing that unless it can be shown that Kastner willed the murder of entire Hungarian Jewry the libel was not justified.

This was also the gist of the argument of Justice Agranat, whose view spans 109 pages. He first argued that since Kastner was accused of murder in the libel, it must be shown as it would in a criminal action that he had a guilty intention [*mens rea*] and had willed this murder. Agranat argued that it has not been proved that Kastner willed the murder of Hungarian Jewry, and that he strove, at every point, to save the largest possible number of Hungarian Jews. He stated his views as follows:

I summarize my final conclusions on Kastner's behaviour during the holocaust of the provincial towns: (1) During that period Kastner was motivated by the sole motive of saving Hungary's Jews as a whole, that is, the largest possible number under the circumstances of time and place as he estimated that could be saved; (2) This motive fitted the moral duty of rescue to which he was subordinated as a leader of the relief and rescue committee in Budapest; (3) Influenced by this motive he adopted the method of financial or economic negotiation with the Nazis; (4) Kastner's behaviour stands the test of plausibility and reasonableness; (5) His behaviour during his visit to Kluj (on May 3rd) and afterwards, both its active aspect (the plan of the 'prominents') and its passive aspect (withholding the 'Auschwitz news' and lack of encouragement for acts of resistance and escape on a large scale) – is in line with his loyalty to the method which he considered, at all important times, to be the only chance for rescue; (6) Therefore one cannot find a moral fault in his behaviour, one cannot discover a causal connection between it and the easing of the concentration and deportation, one cannot see it as becoming a collaboration with the Nazis.[34]

Agranat then used an example given in Ha'levi's judgment about a guard of a camp betraying his duties:

> The enemy informs the guard that the camp is surrounded by superior forces, that it intends to destroy the entire camp and that even if the guard tries to wake his friends they won't manage to escape. The enemy promises the guard to spare the lives of a small number of friends which he may choose on condition that he will not wake all his other friends and not make any attempt to rescue them. The guard presents the enemy with a list of his best friends and avoids alarming the camp and helping it. The enemy destroys the camp and leaves alive only the guard's friends. The guard's act constitutes a betrayal of his friends and duty, collaboration with the enemy, and assistance to destroying the camp (para. 64).

My answer to this example is that it fails to apply to our case for two reasons:

First, the plan of the prominents was never considered by Kastner as a singular rescue mission for whose sake he forsook the rescue of the rest of the Jews in the provinces. It was only a by-product of the negotiations to prevent the deportation of Hungarian Jews as whole, and in his eyes this plan was in line with the plan of maximum rescue and not opposed to it. Second, the duty of the guard in the example above – to alarm the camp on the sudden arrival of the enemy who comes to destroy is a ministerial duty, well defined in advance, from which he couldn't deviate in the slightest. But Kastner's public duty obliged him to care for the rescue of the whole of Hungarian Jewry, in other words his sole moral duty was to aspire to rescue the largest number of Jews it was possible to save. Therefore the decision on the question of whether he had to tell the Jews in the ghettos his actual information depended on his evaluation of the use of this means for the said 'maximal' end. But we saw that his evaluation of this issue – which was reasonable – was negative. Therefore my view is that the president (of the District Court) was wrong in his conclusion that the defendant proved, with regard to the holocaust of the provincial towns in Hungary, his first two charges. The tragedy which these Jews suffered is enormous and horrifying both in its substance and scope. But the proof to substantiate it in this case does not justify the conclusion that Dr. Kastner knowingly contributed to this sad outcome and does not justify that he be stained, accordingly, by the stain of a collaborator with the Nazis.[35]

The law on which Justice Agranat, and all the judges of the Supreme Court, based their considerations was Israeli law for dealing with ordinary criminals. But can a political leader, whose policies prove catastrophic, be judged according to the narrow rules designed to deal with ordinary crimes?

Justice Agranat argued that as long as the aim of saving the majority of Hungary's Jews was foremost in his mind Kastner could be accused neither of 'collaboration with the Nazis' nor of 'preparing the ground for murder'. Judge Kheshin agreed, but added:

> In the moral domain: this is not a question of whether a person be allowed to kill many in order to save a few or vice versa. The question is in a totally different domain, and has to be formulated thus: a person sees that an entire community is doomed; is he allowed to make efforts to save the minority, although some of the efforts consist of hiding the truth from the majority, or must he reveal the truth to all even though to the best of his knowledge all will be destroyed by this?
>
> I think that the answer is clear: what will the blood of the few add to that of the many?
>
> On this point we have the illuminating testimony of Freudiger, that man seen by all as honest, and a capable leader. He was asked by the court a simple question and gave a clear answer:

> Ha'levi: Was it necessary for a Jew who wished to save Jews to study the aims of the Nazis in this trading or was it enough for a Jew to say: every Jewish soul the Nazis allows me to save I save, and if they ask for money I pay money, if they have political or other unknown aims it is none of my business? Or must the Jews answer the question: perhaps in this deal they want to facilitate the extermination of the rest of the Jews?
>
> Freudiger: This is really a very hard question, Mr. President, and I can only answer according to religious law. To my knowledge if it is possible to save a single Jew then one must save him. This is one of the three laws for which one must be ready to die rather than forsake. If I can save someone even if later this will cause worse things to others, then according to my understandinging of religious laws I must save him, whether there is worse to come or not ... If I can save I must save ... according to my understand, he who must save the people, and can save, should save (Freudiger's testimony, 24/53).[36]

Justice Keshin accepts this view. Actually, the next sentence in Freudiger's testimony (which Justice Kheshin failed to quote) says: 'Had someone approached me with the problem as the honourable president formulated it to me I would have asked my rabbinical office what to do.'[37]

Kheshin states:

> No law, national or international, determines the duties of a leader in time of emergency towards those who rely on his leadership and depend on his command. Moreover, there is no law attaching criminal responsibility to a leader. I think we can state explicitly that if we rule that Kastner collaborated with the enemy because he failed to inform those who boarded the trains in Kluj that they were heading for extermination then it is necessary to bring to court today also Dantzig, Herman, Hanzi Brand, Rahbes, and Marton, and many other leaders and half leaders who also kept silent in times of crisis, who didn't inform others about what they knew, who didn't raise the alarm, and didn't warn about the impending danger. Even Freudiger himself, that man of pure conscience and direct manner, will not come clean. If the honourable president was right in his judgment then Kastner deserves death according to the law of judging the Nazis and their collaborators (1950). I refuse to believe that a Jewish judge would pass a death sentence on Kastner and others like him on the basis of the evidence presented in this trial.
>
> For these reasons I cannot accept the conclusions of the lower court on the accusations of the defendant against Kastner on collaboration with the Nazis to exterminate the masses of the Jews in Hungary during the last war.[38]

It is little wonder that the judges in the Supreme Court agreed that the proper forum for judging Kastner's behaviour and policies would be a public enquiry committee. But the government did nothing to set this up.

The Assassination

Even before the Supreme Court heard the appeal, Kastner was assassinated. On the evening of 4 March 1957 he was shot outside his house by Ze'ev Ekstein, who was then driven away by Dan Shemer in a stolen jeep. The police arrested them in their homes that same night. Next morning the police had their confessions. A third man, Joseph Menkes, was arrested a little later. Shemer and Ekstein were former employees of the Israel Secret Service. On the day of the assassination an agent of the Secret Service warned his superiors that the assassination would take place that night. No precautions were taken. Kastner was alive and conscious in hospital for another 12 days. Brand, Kastner's deputy and close friend, wrote:

Perhaps cautious politicians didn't know what to do with one person after his trial, where to 'house' him. Needless to add that the public enquiry committee suggested by the judges of the Supreme Court was never established.[39]

Who Authorised Kastner?

For his actions in both Hungary and Nurenberg Kastner claimed to have the authority of the Jewish Agency. When his statement on behalf of Becher was given he signed as a representative of the Agency and reported to its treasurer. Kastner stated in his testimony to Ha'levi:

Before going to Nurenberg [to testify] I sat with the people of the Jewish Agency and with people from the [Jewish] Congress to discuss what to do to bring the Nazis, particularly those who participated in the extermination of the Jews, to trial. There was also a question of what to do about the few cases in which we received help from the Nazis. I mentioned then especially Becher, and the court knows my opinion on him. I asked if in case of a request to give an opinion on this matter I may say, not only in my name, but also on behalf of the Jewish Agency or the Congress, that he deserves consideration for his help in rescuing the Jews. I got a positive answer.

The trial transcript continues:

Ha'Levi: 'You mentioned Becher's case specifically?'
Kastner: 'Yes. Specifically.'
'With whom did you talk then?'
'With Perlzweig and Ridner of the Jewish Congress and Barlass and Dobkin from the Jewish Agency.'
'And these four people gave the permission.'
'They agreed. Yes.'
'They agreed in relation to Becher specifically?'
'Yes.'
[Dobkin, a member of the Executive Committee of the Jewish Agency, then gave a very short testimony. He was asked to testify on one point only. Did he or did he not give Kastner permission to make a statement of behalf of the Jewish Agency?]
Tamir: 'Mr. Dobkin, when did you first hear the name of the SS officer Kurt Becher?'
Dobkin: 'I met this name for the first time only now, when I read the report about the trial.'
'There is a version that you and Barlass agreed that Kastner should testify on Becher's behalf and even add a recommendation in your name. Do you remember such a thing?'

'No. I don't remember any such thing. I don't remember discussing this subject with him.'

'Did you know that Dr. Kastner was going to Nurenberg to testify?'

'I cannot remember.'

'Did you ever face a moral dilemma for testifying on behalf of a Nazi?'

'No.'

'Were you authorized – as head of the Jewish Organizations Department [in the Agency] – to give permission to testify on behalf of an SS General or Colonel?'

'I had no authority in these matters.'

'Do you remember a debate in the Executive of the Agency on the problem of testifying on behalf of a Nazi?'

'No. I have searched my memory, referred to documents and spoken to Mr. Barlass about it, and failed to recall.'

Tamir: 'Thank you Mr. Dobkin.'[40]

In his book *Satan and the Soul*, published six years after the trial, Joel Brand comments:

> Kastner testified under oath in court that Eiyah Dobkin and Haim Barlass authorized him on behalf of the Agency to testify in Nurenberg on behalf of the SS Colonel Becher. I don't know if this was so or not. But I do know that Dobkin's claim, under oath, that he heard the name Becher for the first time during that trial, and hence couldn't have authorized Kastner to testify on his behalf, is contrary to the facts. In 1944 Dobkin was due, together with the director of J.O.I.N.T., Joe Schwartz, to meet Becher and Kastner in Lisbon. All the preparations for that meeting were made, but at the last moment it was cancelled since the Allies forbade their citizens to meet with a representative of the Nazis. Therefore, by the way, the dealing with Becher was transferred from Dobkin and Schwartz to Sally Meyer, who was a Swiss citizen. In addition, Dobkin was, with Greenbaum, also the head of the central relief and rescue committee in Jerusalem, one of whose main duties was to meet Kurt Becher and follow the progress of the negotiations with the Nazis. The name of SS Colonel Becher was one of the names mentioned more than others and Dobkin was one of those who knew more than most. I myself spoke to him on the day of my release by the British [having been arrested on bringing Eichmann's offer of 'lorries in exchange for Jews', in 1944] in his office and flat in Jerusalem. He offered me then to come with me to Lisbon to meet Becher. Dobkin's testimony, that he had never heard the name Becher, strengthened my doubts, about whether the central institutions, despite the fact that the Attorney

General personally took over the defence of Rezso, were really interested in clearing him.[41]

Brand mentions in his book that when Tamir met him privately, to ask him to testify in the Kastner trial, he replied:

> Mr. Tamir, I have such horrifying and incriminating material against the heads of the [Jewish] State – who were the heads of the Jewish Agency at the time – that would shock the entire state. They simply cannot afford to allow such material to become public knowledge. If I testify blood will flow in the streets of Tel-Aviv, therefore I doubt whether it is desirable from a national point of view.

Tamir smiled with sad irony and said:

> You don't know the Jewish community Mr. Brand. Not a single window will be smashed as a result of your testimony. That is perhaps the worst tragedy that has happened to us, the senses have been dulled, the national body doesn't respond normally even to the most painful blows.[42]

Eventually Brand testified, and not a window was smashed. On one occasion he was driving home with Ehud Avriel, the representative of the Political Department of the Jewish Agency, headed by M. Sharett during 1944, and who was instrumental in handing Brand over to the British when he arrived from Budapest. Avriel commented on Brand's book: 'I understand that you wish, and even must, tell the truth, but bear in mind that it is the tone which makes the music. It is not necessary to tell everything. In fact, we should all have been put up against the wall [and shot].'[43]

In the 1980s a campaign to rehabilitate Kastner started in Israel. It culminated, on 26 July 1993, in a decision proposed by Mayor Shlomo Lahat to the Tel Aviv city council, to name a street after Kastner. The resolution was passed by a considerable majority.

Notes and References

1. First published in *Perdition*, 1987, London: Ithaca Press.
2. *Personal Diary of Moshe Sharett* (Hebrew), 1978, vol. 2, p. 376, Tel-Aviv: Ma'ariv.
3. *The Sentence of the District Court in Jerusalem on Case 124/53: The Attorney General against Malkiel Greenwald before the President of the Court Dr Benjamin Ha'levi* (Hebrew), 1956, Tel-Aviv: Karni, p. 38.
4. *The sentence*, p. 45.
5. *Personal Diary*, vol. 4, p. 1,073.
6. Eugene Levai, *The Black Book on the Martyrdom of Hungarian Jewry*, 1948, Vienna: Panorama, p. 418.

7.   *The Black Book*, p. 187.
8.   S. Rosenfeld, *Criminal Case 124, the Greenwald-Kastner Trial* (Hebrew) 1955, Tel-Aviv: Karni, p. 101.
9.   Rudolf Vrba, 'Footnote to Auschwitz Report', in *Jewish Currents*, March 1966, p. 22.
10. Rosenfeld, *Criminal Case 124*, p. 100.
11. *Criminal Case 124, The Verdict*, p. 44.
12. *Criminal Case, The Verdict*, p. 47.
13. *Criminal Case, The Verdict*, p. 47.
14. *Criminal Case, The Verdict*, p. 50.
15. *Criminal Case, The Verdict*, p. 50.
16. *Criminal Case, The Verdict*, pp. 54–55.
17   *Criminal Case, The Verdict*, 123.
18. *Criminal Case, The Verdict*, p. 153.
19   *Criminal Case, The Verdict*, p. 168.
20. *The Black Book*, p. 272.
21. *The Judgment*, p. 204.
22. *Criminal Case 124, The Verdict*, p. 254.
23. *Judgments of the Supreme [Appeal] Court in Israel* (Hebrew), 1958, vol. 79, Jerusalem: State Publishing House, p. 2,210.
24. *Judgments*, p. 2,210.
25. *Criminal Case 124, The Verdict*, p. 204.
26. *Criminal Case 124, The Verdict*, p. 206.
27. Joel and Hansi Brand, *Satan and the Soul* (Hebrew), 1960, Tel-Aviv: Ledori, p. 107.
28. *Satan*, p. 6
29. *Satan*, p. 7
30. *Satan*, pp. 8-9.
31. *Verdicts of the Supreme [Appeal] Court*, 1958, vol. 83, p. 2,315.
32. *Verdicts*, vol. 82, p. 2,279.
33. *Verdicts*, vol. 81, p. 2,251.
34. *Verdicts*, vol. 78, p. 2,176.
35. *Verdicts*, vol. 78, p. 2,179.
36. *Verdicts*, vol. 83, p. 2,302.
37. *Criminal Case 124*, p. 37.
38. *Verdicts*, vol. 83, p. 2,309.
39. *Satan*, p. 209.
40. *Criminal Case 124*, p. 256.
41. *Satan*, p. 146.
42. *Satan*, p. 128.
43. *Satan*, p. 138.

Part Three

ETHNICITY

Introduction: Politics of Ethnic Identity

The collapse of the USSR, an event to which there is nothing comparable in history, exposed to a stunned world a welter of nationalistic conflicts whose ferocity and cruelty were totally unexpected at the end of the twentieth century. As if to press the point that this was no aberration there followed the collapse of Yugoslavia. It seems clear that the education systems of these two states failed (if they ever tried) to neutralise ethnic strife.

Some people believe that ethnic conflicts are the fault of power-hungry politicians who fan them for their own ends. In many cases there are facts to substantiate this argument, but it fails to account for the existence of ethnic loyalties. Power-hungry politicians exploit various kinds of loyalty, they don't create them. In India religious obsessions produce feuds that are exploited by certain politicians; in many African states the feuds are tribal. Racist attitudes can be discerned in almost any country in the world. Exploiters have a vested interest in perpetuating the anxieties on which they feed. The difficult part is overcoming them. All these conflicts have much in common. Each has its unique features and history. But the psychological and political dynamics of each are very similar. Insights gained by studying one are useful in dealing with all.

One of the oldest nationalisms, which has been reactivated after a political hibernation of 2,000 years, is the Jewish one. Secular Jewish nationalism, known as 'political Zionism' (to distinguish it from cultural, religious or emotional Zionism), emerged as a political force in 1897 in Europe. Its aim was to establish a Jewish, secular nation-state. Its founder, Theodore Herzl, was willing to establish that state anywhere – in the Argentine, in Uganda, wherever. His followers insisted on 'Palestine' (whose biblical name, 'Zion', gave the movement its name). The implementation of the aim caused bitter conflict with the indigenous population of Palestine, namely Arabs who had inhabited Palestine since the seventh century (many were probably descendants of the ancient Israelites ...). The Palestinian Arabs, an absolute majority, outnumbering the Jews in Palestine by ten to one in 1920, had their own aspirations for independence. The ensuing conflict in Palestine – as in Northern Ireland – was and is between the immigrant settlers who insist on various legally enshrined, ethnic privileges, and the indigenous population. This is no ordinary colonial conflict. Economic advantages are not its main motivation. The dominant anxiety motivating the secular Zionists is not economic but psychological. They feel threatened and are convinced they defend their 'survival'. As in Northern Ireland, 'survival' not of their physical existence but survival of their identity as a group. Jewish group identity is indeed threatened, but the threat is an inner one due to secularisation. Jewish ethnicity depends on Jewish religion. Politics cannot help here. People with a secure group identity (like Orthodox religious Jews) do not feel they are fighting for survival even when their physical life is threatened.

Jewish nationalism can serve as a useful case study to reveal the dynamics of ethnic conflicts for a number of reasons:

1. Jews are one of the oldest ethnic groups in the world, and have a well-documented history both as persecuted and persecutors
2. the Zionist conflict with Palestinian nationalism has been thoroughly documented
3. in the state of Israel itself there is an internal conflict between humanists and nationalists
4. the unique feature of Jewish ethnicity is the nature of its link with the Jewish religion – when Jews cease to practise their religion their ethnic identity becomes enigmatic, this produces a conflict between secular Jews, who are the majority in Israel, and the Orthodox religious Jewish minority there.

A popular Jewish proverb says: 'when thieves quarrel truth is revealed'. Likewise, when secular Jewish nationalists and Orthodox religious Jews quarrel (as they do all the time in Israel) they reveal truths about each other which they will never reveal or admit to outsiders. Much of what can be learnt from these revelations is useful in combating nationalism generally.

Nationalism is an ethnocentric value system. It grants highest priority to the interests of a particular ethnic group (however one defines these interests). This group can be a tribe, a clan, a nation, a race, etc. Anyone who says *'my country, right or wrong'*, *'my race/tribe/clan above all else'*, *'my nation comes first'*, or expresses readiness *'to die for king and country'* accepts the ethnocentric value system, and is – by definition – a nationalist, tribalist, racist.

Humanism is a different value system. It puts the interests of humanity as a whole (however one defines them) before any interest of any human group, and even before one's own personal interests. Such a value system is known as anthropocentric. International socialism (not some national version) and Paul's Christianity (not some churchianity) are anthropocentric value systems. Antropocentrism and ethnocentrism exclude each other. A person cannot uphold two different value systems. When a decision has to be taken, and the value systems guiding the choice are in conflict, one value system must prevail. Most people in the West nowadays accept an egocentric value system (priority is given to one's own interests), believing it to be 'sensible', or 'rational' and the other values to be 'irrational', 'unnatural'. This is a common fallacy. Value systems are not comparable because the yardsticks by which they measure everything are part of the value system. There are no 'objective' yardsticks – outside all value systems – for comparing value systems. It is, however, imperative to understand a vewpoint totally different from one's own if one wishes to relate to it in a manner that will be effective.

In conflicts between tribes, or nations, nationalists insist that the interests of their clan, tribe, nation, have priority over all else including an individual life. They join the fray. Humanists insist that people of all groups have common interests and refuse to join one group against another. Some people find that when they are facing ethnic confrontations their feelings contradict their convictions – they believe they are humanists but are swept away by their nationalist feelings. This has happened to many socialists during the last 80 years.

Socialists have dealt with nationalist movements in three ways:

1. by trying to combine socialism and nationalism
2. by labelling nationalism as 'false consciousness'
3. by applying the political principle of 'the right of nations to self-determination'.

All three have produced negative, even disastrous, results.

Combining nationalism with socialism has produced various brands of national-socialism culminating in Hitler's Germany and Mussolini's Italy.

To label a human trait as 'false' obscures its structure, thus obstructing efforts to overcome it.

To elevate the nationalist demand for political independence to the rank of an unconditionally accepted 'right' deprives the humanists and socialists of a guiding principle in the political struggle against nationalism. This has been proved again and again in a century littered with failures of the socialist movement to overcome nationalistic politics. Socialists reject 'the right of races (or tribes) to self-determination'; but replace 'races' (or 'tribes') by 'nations' and we get the political principle which guides socialists in their response to the nationalistic demand for a nation-state.

Instead of challenging the right to political independence based on ethnicity, they accept it. In this way they contribute and prolong – inadvertently – the ethnic conflicts they fight against.

In the struggle against nationalistic politics socialists and humanists ought to follow the principles they accept for dealing with all ethnocentric politics, be they racial, religious, tribal, or sexual, namely: *separation of ethnicity from the state*. This means that the laws of any state must not grant privileges to any particular group and must punish those who discriminate against any group. This is accepted with regard to tribal, racial, religious and sexual groups, and ought to be extended to ethnic groups as well.

The essays in this segment deal with issues of ethnic identity and nationalism and the related politics, from an anthropocentric viewpoint opposing the ethnocentric one. They should help the reader to gain a better understanding of the dynamics of ethnic conflicts in general, and thus contribute to overcoming them.

10

Whose Right to Self-determination[1]

Most contemporary socialists take it for granted that the 'right to national self-determination' is a progressive demand. We see them waving Viet Cong flags or proclaiming their 'full solidarity with the IRA'. They seem to believe that 'the enemies of my enemies must necessarily be my friends', forgetting in the process the class nature of politics.

This essay urges a return to a principled humanism. It will doubtless annoy those who believe 'activity' can proceed without previous thought as to where one wants to go. As for us, we would rather struggle for what we want – even if we don't immediately get it – than struggle for what we don't want ... and get it.

Why further discussion on the national problem? Anyone familiar with the voluminous literature on this issue over the past century ought to ask this question. First there was the Marx-Proudhon controversy over the national struggle of the Poles. Then came Marx's conflicting views on the Irish question. At the turn of the century we have the Lenin-Luxemburg controversy on the question of self-determination for the Poles in particular, and for oppressed national minorities in general.

These are merely the better-known writings on the subject. Hundreds of lesser known pamphlets and articles have circulated in every socialist organisation throughout the world. And if, despite all this, there is still a sufficient readership in the movement to justify the publication of another text on the subject, it can only mean that what *has been said* in the past has failed to provide a satisfying answer.

The reason for the uneasiness felt by many socialists concerning the national question is not hard to discern. Every socialist, including those who uphold the right to self-determination on a national basis, agrees that nationalism was a bourgeois ideology. Its modern form, which has been an active political force over the past 300 years, was born with the bourgeoisie and served its political, economic and social interests. It is also agreed in the left that the struggle *against* national discrimination, oppression and persecution is an integral part of the struggle for socialism. The differences have been about the right of the persecuted minority to establish a nation-state.

The demand to establish an independent nation-state was a banner under which masses of people were mobilised to struggle against oppression. Anyone who remained silent on this issue or opposed this demand (for whatever reason) antagonised broad masses of people, mostly workers and peasants, who were sincerely struggling against oppression. These struggles were never struggles for abolishing national discrimination as such. Many of them were motivated by the belief that 'minority persecution is inherent in human nature'. They aimed at creating separate nation-states in which the persecuted minority would become the dominant majority. They did not aim to oppress other minorities, they merely aimed at establishing their own nation as the dominant one. That is why all national liberation movements always demanded separation from the national group which constituted the majority and political independence (to establish a political, economic and legal system that would safeguard their national majority and their privileges).

No struggle waged under the banner of national liberation ever created a regime which abolished national discrimination – these struggles merely transformed a discriminated minority into a discriminating majority. To be sure, these struggles also had broader repercussions. They weakened the particular imperialist power against which they were directed, whether it was the Poles struggling against Tsarism, the Greeks against the Ottoman Empire, the Irish against British imperialism, or the Indonesians against Dutch rule. But this weakening of the political grip of an imperial power was made under the banner of the bourgeois ideology of nationalism, which explicitly demands the subordination of class interests to national (bourgeois) interest.

This has contributed to the entrenchment of regimes deeply permeated by nationalistic ideology. In the last 25 years millions of people in Asia and Africa have waged struggles against imperialism and for self-determination, yet wherever the demand for self-determination has been dominated by nationalist ideology it has produced regimes opposed to social revolution. To argue that this is a 'necessary phase' in the development towards social revolution is to seek cover behind a grand scheme of 'historical necessity'.

What is necessary and what is not necessary in history? Was the emergence of Pilsudski's Poland and of Mannerheim's Finland a 'historical necessity'? Was de Valera's Ireland a 'historical necessity'? Is an independent state of black Americans, inside or outside the USA, a 'historical necessity'? Is a Jewish state in the Middle East a 'historical necessity'? Was Castro's victory in Cuba a 'historical necessity'? Was Mao's victory over Chiang Kai-shek a 'historical necessity'? Is the role of revolutionaries merely to hasten the realisation of what is anyway a 'historical necessity'? Was May 1968 in France – and its political aftermath – a 'historical necessity'? And if so, why did those who think so not foresee this historical necessity in April 1968? Let those who mobilise the argument of 'historical necessity' in defence of their policies go on acting as a passive midwife to an active historical process. We prefer to play the role of begetter. To each his rationalisation and to each his reward.

It has been argued – defensively – by Lenin and his followers, that:

> recognition of the right of nations to separation does not contradict propaganda against separation by Marxists of the oppressed nation, just as the recognition of the right to divorce does not contradict propaganda, in this or that case, against divorce. To accuse the supporters of the right to self-determination (i.e. the right to separation) of advocating separation is the same stupidity and hypocrisy as to accuse the supporters of the right to divorce of the destruction of family relations. [2]

This analogy between the right to divorce and the right to self-determination on an ethnic basis, which is brought up repeatedly by Leninists, is misleading and obscures the issue. The right to divorce is a right to dissolve a relationship. It makes no reference to the situation of the divorcee after the divorce. The right of self-determination based on ethnicity emphasises precisely the acceptance of a particular mode of political existence *after* the separation.

I do not argue that Lenin and his supporters accepted nationalism. I am fully aware that their insistence on upholding the principle of the right of nations to self-determination was motivated by their belief that this policy would help overcome the nationalism of the oppressed people and help win them over to internationalism and socialism. The question is (judging today and with the wisdom of hindsight), whether this policy was right or wrong. What did it in fact help to bring about? Were its expectations justified? Or were they refuted? And concerning the recent past and the emergence of independent nation-states in Asia and Africa, from Pakistan to Nigeria and from Cyprus to Ceylon, does the support which the left gave to the right of *nations* to self-determination not imply a certain responsibility for what these states turned out to be, when they finally won the struggle – not only in terms of their internal policies but also in terms of their role in international politics?

Let me clarify my criticism and forestall misinterpretations. I distinguish between the struggle *against* ethnic oppression and the struggle *for* political independence based on ethnicity. The first is part of the struggle for a society which has abolished all discrimination. The second is a struggle to change roles within existing society. It is often said that such abstract arguments are meaningless unless they are applied to an actual, concrete case. And yet on issues like racial or religious dicrimination no concrete struggle will ever make a socialist uphold the principle of right to self-determination based on religion or race. Under what circumstances would a socialist uphold the demand of a religiously or racially persecuted minority to establish an independent state based on its *religion* or *race*?

It goes without saying that every socialist must struggle against religious and racial discrimination. But here the struggle *against* does not imply upholding the right *for* establishing a political system based on the race or religion of the persecuted.

Socialists accept the policy of 'separation of religion from the state' and 'separation of race from the state'. Why then do many of them reject the policy of 'separation of ethnicity from the state'?[3] This last formula, by the way, is effective against both the nationalism of the oppressor and against the (understandable) nationalism of the oppressed.

I do not consider these two to be symmetrical politically. But while struggling against the oppressing nationalism, we must not advocate the right of self-determination based on nationalism. To uphold this as an inalienable 'right' is to make a major concession to the nationalistic ideology, to accept its legitimacy.

Revolutionaries might decide *as a matter of political tactics* to support a struggle for self-determination waged by a persecuted ethnic minority. But when it comes to advocating a *right* they ought to advocate one right only: the right of workers councils to self-determination. Nowadays any deviation from this principle, any acceptance of 'rights of nations', 'national interest', etc. by socialists is tantamount to capitulating to the nationalist bourgeoisie or bureaucracy. This is the lesson we can learn from upholding the principle of the right of *nations* to self-determination over the last 70 years.

Notes and References

1. Published in *Solidarity*, vol. 7, no. 1, 1972.
2. Lenin, 'On the Right of Nations to Self-Determination', *Selected Works*, 1952, Moscow: State Publishing House, vol. 1, part 2.
3. By 'separation from the state' I mean that the laws of the state confer no privileges to any racial, religious or ethnic group, and punish anyone who discriminates against others because of their religion, race or ethnic origin.

11

State and Ethnicity in Palestine[1]

A New Situation – New Problems

The appearance of the PLO Chairman before the General Assembly of the UN in November 1974 gave the opportunity to 89 out of the 138 governments represented in the UN to express their public and direct support for Palestinian aspirations to political independence. Only eight governments instructed their representatives to vote against the resolution expressing this recognition, and 37 preferred to abstain. In other words: the Palestinians are no longer considered merely as a social problem, as refugees who have lost homes and lands, but are recognised as a political factor, as a population with accepted demands for political independence.

This international recognition of their political status was an important victory for the Palestinians and a shattering defeat to the Israeli policy. Israel has not yet recovered from this defeat and has not managed to shape a new foreign policy adapted to the new situation in international politics. The 'Palestinian problem' has become the 'Israeli problem'. The Palestinians put forward positive proposals, the Israelis reject them. The Israelis now have to explain why they reject the idea of a democratic, secular state in Palestine.

Recognition of the Palestinians as a political entity was also a victory for the anti-Zionist left in Israel, which had fought for this recognition since 1948. This left, which was attacked in hysterical tones by the entire Israeli media, proved not only its moral integrity but also the validity of its political analysis. All the 'Arab specialists' of the Israeli establishment, all its 'think tanks' and 'brain trusts' failed to foresee what a handful of Israeli anti-Zionists had predicted for years – the re-emergence of the Palestinians as a political factor and the slow but inevitable decline of Zionist policies.

However, the content of the speech of the PLO Chairman at the UN also created a new problem for the anti-Zionist left in Israel. Arafat proposed the establishment of a single, joint Jewish-Arab state in Palestine rather than an independent Palestine next to Israel in the territories now under Israeli occupation. This proposal created an unprecedented and unexpected dilemma for the anti-Zionist left in Israel, a dilemma that is not merely political but also emotional and ideological.

For many years the Israeli anti-Zionist left insisted that there are two national entities in Palestine – the Israeli Jews and the Palestinian Arabs, both deserving the 'right of nations to self-determination'. It based its policies on the principle of 'mutual recognition of the national rights of both people'. The anti-Zionist left in Israel never contemplated the possibility that the Palestinians would aspire to implement their political aspirations in a joint, Jewish-Arab state. Instead it was assumed that the Palestinians would establish a separate Arab state and that Israel would have to make the necessary territorial and political concessions.

At present, neither the Israeli government nor the majority of the Israeli public are ready to recognise the Palestinians as a political entity let alone make any territorial or political concessions. The Israeli government opposes anything which implies political recognition of the Palestinians. In the struggle against this policy inside Israel the anti-Zionist left can restrict its argument to the point that the Israelis cannot deny to the Palestinians what they demand for themselves, namely political recognition and independence. Outside Israel, however, the Palestinian argument has won (which does not mean that it will be implemented without further struggle), and a new debate has started concerning the form in which the aspirations of the Palestinians should be implemented. The Palestinians themselves are divided into those who are ready to accept a separate Arab Palestine next to Israel, and those who are willing to carry the struggle further, to a creation of a common non-discriminatory state. The struggle over this issue has already divided the PLO and brought about the creation of the 'rejection front'.

The anti-Zionist left in Israel has not stated its view on this issue. It argues that this is an internal Palestinian matter. Now, for the first time, the left faces a conflict between its ideological principles and political aspirations. The Palestinians, whose right to self-determination was always recognised by the left, propose to implement their right by the creation of a joint, non-discriminatory, Jewish-Arab state. This is a proposal which the Israeli anti-Zionist left supports, although it would add that such a state must be socialist, and part of a larger political system including most of the Middle East. The Israeli people, whose right to self-determination has also been defended by the left, insist on implementing this right in a state that discriminates in favour of Jews. This form of implementation has always been rejected by the left.

Thus, while feeling that the Palestinian proposal is closer to its own aspirations, the anti-Zionist left in Israel finds itself obliged to defend the right of the Israeli population to implement a form of self-determination which it rejects. Aspirations to create a non-discriminatory, multi-national socialist state, are in conflict with the right of nations to self-determination which implies that the national aspirations of a population must be respected as a matter of principle. At the same time the left has no principle with which to express its own aspirations on the national question. It assumed that the national problems would disappear with the disappearance of the private ownership of the means of production – a separate socialist principle to deal with the national problem was therefore unnecessary. However, the existence of national problems in countries where private ownership of the means of production was abolished decades ago indicates that the situation is more complex.

Nationalism remains a force motivating people decades after the abolition of private ownership. Social ownership may weaken the force of national feelings and aspirations, it does not abolish them. That being so it is necessary to formulate a special, socialist principle for dealing with the national problem. It is also necessary to examine the principle which socialists shared with bourgeois nationalists in dealing with the problem, namely the right of nations to self-determination.

Critical Comments on the Right of Nations to Self-determination

'Self-determination of nations means the political separation of these nations from alien national bodies, the formation of independent nation states.'[2] This is the clear and unambiguous definition which Lenin gave to the concept of self-determination of nations, and it is this definition which is accepted by all those who share Lenin's view on the subject. Lenin continues:

> The resolution of the [Second] International [on the national question] reproduces the most essential, the fundamental propositions of this point of view: on the one hand, the absolutely direct, unequivocal recognition of the full right of all nations to self-determination; on the other hand, the equally unambiguous appeal to the workers for international unity, in their class struggle. We think that this resolution is absolutely correct, and that for the countries of Eastern Europe and Asia in the beginning of the twentieth century it is precisely this resolution, in both its parts taken as an inseparable whole, that gives the only correct lead to the proletarian class policy on the national question.[3]

Although Lenin qualified his approach to Eastern Europe and Asia at the beginning of the twentieth century, no one who accepts it has yet proposed a different principle for, say, Africa, in the second half of the century. That is hardly a surprise; for if a policy is elevated to the rank of a principle it becomes much harder to modify it. After all, a principle is not something which is reconsidered every time it has to be applied. Lenin was aware that the modern nation-state is a product of the bourgeoisie, and that the national ideology is part of bourgeois ideology. He supported the aspirations to national independence as a principle because it meant three things to him:

1. unconditional struggle against national oppression
2. the freedom of a national group to separate from an oppressive state
3. non-interference in the manner in which a national group chooses to exercise its political aspirations.

In this manner he hoped to wean the working class, both of the oppressed and of the oppressing nations, away from nationalism. In fact it is possible to struggle against oppression (be it ethnic, racial, religious or sexual) and for the freedom of separation without resorting to 'rights' to self-determination based on ethnicity, race, religion or gender.

Does the struggle against racial discrimination and oppression imply a principle of the 'right of races to self-determination'? Certainly not. There may be some among an oppressed race who will aspire to establish political independence based on their own race, but there is no need for socialists to elevate such an aspiration to the rank of a 'right'. The same applies to problems of religious discrimination. If one rejects the demand to support an aspiration to political independence based on religion or race as a matter of 'right', why then make an exception when it comes to ethnicity?

Lenin compares the support for the right of nations to self-determination to the support for the right to divorce. This comparison reveals the problem. Support for the right to divorce implies neutrality towards the way in which the divorcees choose to live their lives after the separation. Similarly, support for the right of nations to self-determination implies neutrality towards the manner in which the separated groups choose to establish their political systems after the separation. But can a socialist remain neutral towards a political system based on ethnicity (race or religion)? Certainly not.

No wonder, therefore, that people like Rosa Luxemburg and Trotsky argued against Lenin's view on this issue. No wonder either that although Lenin quotes Marx's comments supporting the struggle for national independence of the Irish and the Poles, he cannot find reference to the 'right' of nations to self-determination in Marx.

Quite apart from the fact that the principle of the right of nations to self-determination renders it very difficult to oppose demands for political independence based on ethnicity even in cases where there is no doubt that this demand is detrimental to socialist politics, the acceptance of the principle has ideological implications. This principle, in its historical origin and political significance, is a bourgeois principle; its acceptance by socialists implies an ideological concession to the class enemy. A mere rejection of this principle is not enough. An alternative principle is required to serve the needs of revolutionary ideas and politics.

Separation of Ethnicity from the State[4]

Separation of ethnicity from the state means a political and legal system which neither grants nor denies rights on the basis of ethnicity, and is designed to prevent ethnic discrimination and oppression. The principle of separation of ethnicity from the state has a number of implications:

1. it contributes to the liberation of socialist mentality from the residues of bourgeois ideology (for example, 'national rights')
2. it implies a critique of concepts like 'national interest', 'national loyalty', and national historiography
3. it challenges the ideology of the national oppressor while immunising the oppressed against nationalism
4. it exposes connections between social emotions, views, and political systems
5. it challenges not only a regime based on ethnic discrimination, but also on ideology in which such discrimination is latent
6. it draws a clear dividing line between socialists and oppressed nationalists even when they wage a joint struggle against a common oppressor
7. it enables socialists to relate to movements for political independence on their own merit, according to their relation to the revolutionary process
8. it helps shift the struggle against national oppression from its national objective towards the socialist objective.

This principle forces those who reject it to clarify, to themselves and to others, why they oppose the separation of ethnicity (however one wishes to define it) from the state. In other words, the entire issue of the relationship between state and ethnicity (between political authority and ethnic identity) is raised anew, whereas hitherto it was taken for granted as something 'natural' or a product of some 'historical necessity'.

In the particular case of Israel, the secular Jewish majority which supports the demand for the separation of religion from the state while opposing the separation of ethnicity from the state will be forced to examine the dependence of its secular nationalism on religion. Nationalism or patriotism may be a substitute for religion but why must a secular Jewish state be located in biblical Zion? Religion – No; ethnicity based on religion – Yes?

The principle of separating the state from ethnicity does not hinder the struggle against occupation, national discrimination and oppression; it imposes no limitation on the freedom of separation – all these being products of an ethnic political system. While enabling one to struggle against these the principle shifts the emphasis of the struggle towards the source which produced them, by challenging the ethnic state and ideology which produce occupation, ethnic oppression and aspirations for separation in an oppressed ethnic group.

Comments on the Application of the Principle

A general principle can guide political activity, it does not necessarily provide solutions to actual problems. Actual solutions depend on actual circumstances. In applying the principle to the Israeli–Arab conflict in Palestine we must take into account the fact that the Israeli Jews constitute a national minority in the middle east and will remain so after the defeat of Zionism, and after redressing the wrongs inflicted on the Palestinians. The fear of minority status should be taken into account in any solution to such long-standing conflicts. The basic democratic principle of 'one person – one vote' is inadequate for relieving the understandable anxiety of a potential minority. In such cases it is necessary to supplement the principle of 'majority rule' by an additional constitutional principle that will defend the national, racial or religious minority from being discriminated against by the majority. Such a principle will state simply: no right will be granted to an ethnic, racial or religious majority unless it be granted also to the corresponding minority. In other words, whatever the majority enjoys, the minority enjoys as well. Such a constitutional principle, if accepted by all, can form the basis for a new political system and new relations between ethnic, racial or religious groups with a long history of strife and conflict.

Many will argue that such a principle is unrealistic, that it does not provide sufficient guarantee, that it cannot be implemented. The question is whether those who put forward these objections consider the principle as desirable. Those who consider it desirable will, eventually, make it practical. Those who, deep down, consider such a principle undesirable should say so openly rather than take refuge behind arguments about practicality.

Constitutional guarantees alone will not abolish all actual practice of ethnic, racial or religious discrimination. However, they form a basis for ideological and educational struggle against discrimination.

Some Specific Features of our Historical Period

Lenin reminds us that:

The categorical demand of Marxist theory in examining any social question is that the question be examined within definite historical limits, and if it refers to a particular country (eg the national programme for a particular country) that due account be taken of the specific features that distinguish that country from others within the same historical epoch.[5]

Clearly, the tremendous innovations in the means of warfare, comunication and production in the last 30 years have put the whole issue of national independence in a new perspective. What does independence mean to all those who depend for economic and military aid on one of the superpowers? Is it the freedom to choose which superpower to depend on? Nuclear weapons and ballistic missiles, TV and the transistor radio, the computer and automated production are powerful factors driving the separate nation-states into larger, supernational, common economic and political frameworks. Participation in such frameworks requires surrender of many components of national independence. Since the defeat of colonialism in Africa and Asia most countries there enjoy political independence. Yet most independent countries find themselves dependent economically or militarily on a superpower. Whatever one may think of it, the full political independence of the nation-state is a thing of the past. The general historical trend, and I consider it positive, is to break out of the national constraints rather than to build them up. In this modern historical context the principle of separation of ethnicity from the state is certainly no less 'realistic' than the right of nations to self-determination.

Specific Features of Political Zionism and the State of Israel

The state of Israel, the colonisatory process which brought it into existence, its institutions, policies, economy and society are the creations of political Zionism. This organisation strove to create a nation-state in Palestine for all Jews throughout the world. How one labels it matters little. What matter are its actual features:

1. Israel was based entirely on immigration of Jews to Palestine, unlike other states based on indigenous populations
2. Zionist immigration – unlike other migratory movements – was motivated by the political aim of creating a Jewish nation-state in Palestine
3. the Zionist settlers in Palestine were a minority aspiring to create an exclusivist Jewish state in a territory where the indigenous majority was Arab
4. the Zionist immigrants could not enter Palestine without permission of the imperial power which ruled it, nor could they implement their aspirations unless they corresponded

to those of the imperial power, therefore Zionism co-operated with the Ottoman rulers of Palestine, and later with the British

5. Israel in its Zionist form has governments which have a pro-imperialist foreign policy, and whose army depends on the USA for military equipment – its entire economy depends on grants and loans from the West

6. Zionism did not aspire to create an independent state for the people of Palestine, nor even for the Jews actually living there; its aim was, and remains, to maintain a state for every Jew in the world, granting automatic rights of immigration and 'return' to anyone who qualifies as a 'Jew'

7. though political Zionism is a secular movement, it is motivated by national sentiments fuelled by religion, hence the insistence on immigration to biblical Zion

8. the main motivation of Zionism is the quest for identity of secular Jewry. Hence the vehement opposition to assimilation and mixed marriages inside and outside Israel

9. Israel is a secular state, but as there is no generally accepted secular definition of the term 'Jew' there can be no legal definition of the term 'Jew', hence the dependence on religion, and on anti-Jewish hostility, to define a 'Jew'.

These features outline the inevitability of conflict with the indigenous Palestinian population. Only by expropriating the Palestinians and opposing their aspirations to independence could Zionism achieve its aim. The dependence of Zionist ideology on national identity linked to religion brought about the political and legal dependence of the secular Israeli majority on the religious minority in Israel. All Israeli governments, dominated by the Zionist labour movement which considers itself socialist and atheist, refused to separate religion from the state.

Despite the fact that the contribution of the Zionist movement to the revolutionary processes in the Middle East and elsewhere has been negative, the revolutionary left has dealt with it exclusively by means of the principle of the right of nations to self-determination. The Palestine Communist Party argued, from the early 1920s to 1948, that the Jews, in Israel and elsewhere, do not constitute 'a nation' and therefore do not qualify for self-determination. The PCP analysis argued that in Palestine there exists a Jewish minority within an Arab nation. However, when the Communist movement changed its analysis in 1948, and stated that in Palestine there are two nations, one Arab and one Jewish, it immediately supported the demand for self-determination to both nations despite the assessment that Zionism was inherently reactionary. This is not the only case where adherence to the principle of the right of nations to self-determination has forced political organisations to support national movements they have considered harmful to the local and global revolutionary process.

The debate as to whether the Israeli Jews and Palestinian-Arabs qualify for the title of 'nation' stems largely from adherence to the principle of the right of nations to self-determination. Only according to this principle has any group which qualifies as a 'nation' the 'right' to establish its own nation-state.

Those who accept the principle of the separation of ethnicity from the state can channel their energy to deal with the nature of the state and its relation to the national problem. When dealing with Israel this implies the following:

1. abolition of the regulations requiring Israeli citizens to register by ethnic origin
2. abolition of the immigration law which grants automatic immigration rights to any Jew, while denying them to non-Jews
3. abolition of the citizenship law which grants automatic citizenship to any Jew, while denying it to non-Jews, including Palestinians who have lived in Israel all their life but are missing on a certain census day
4. abolition of all regulations, laws and practices which deny rights to Arab citizens while granting them to Jews
5. separation of religion from the state, civil marital law and burial services
6. legislation against any practice of discrimination by ethnicity, religion, race or sex.

These demands supplement the demands for withdrawal from all territories occupied in 1967, honouring the demands of the Palestinian refugees for repatriation and compensation, changing foreign policy to support struggles for socialism in the Arab world, etc. The new state should strive to contribute to the struggles for revolution throughout the region, to create a new society and become an integral part of it. The basic problem for the Israeli Jews is not the 'existence' of the state but the nature of that existence. A state based on discrimination between Jew and non-Jew is a reactionary system and must be defeated. A state that separates religion, race and ethnicity from the political apparatus is one that is worth struggling for.

Some Features of Arab Society

For over a century Arab society has been in a deep and protracted political, social and ideological crisis. This crisis is a result of the impact of modern capitalism. Until the 1960s the crisis was obscured by the struggle against the direct military and political presence of

Britain and France. But even after the abolition of direct imperialist rule, and since the achievement of political independence in most Arab countries, the crisis has continued. The present crisis is expressed mainly in the nature of the independent Arab regimes, in the form in which a tiny clique, often a handful of officers, has appropriated all political authority, and in the manner in which it deals with social problems. The background for this crisis is the fact that the vast majority of the population in the Arab world is dominated by religion. Islam includes a detailed legal code which is official law in many Arab countries. The role of women, as well as attitudes to the family, education and social change are deeply influenced by religion. Its influence on the vast masses of people is similar to the influence of Christianity on the European masses in the Middle Ages. However, Europe underwent a prolonged ideological and cultural struggle against religion in the sixteenth and seventeenth centuries when the merchants, bankers and artisans (the bourgeoisie and city-zen) struggled against the political domination of the landed aristocracy and the religious authority of the Church. The victory of science, and its entrenchment as a world outlook, paved the way for the political revolutions of the bourgeoisie, and for the industrial revolution. This internal struggle between social classes transformed European society. Such a struggle did not occur in the Arab world. There was no significant class of landed aristocracy in the Mashreq. Most of the land in the Mashreq was owned by the state, which leased it, via its officials, to the peasantry. Often, the officials were city merchants. The absence of an internal class struggle implied the absence of social change, development and innovation. The innovations came from outside, from Europe, in a manner designed to further the interests of European capitalism rather than to transform the Arab society. Clearly, a religious faith, which has hardly changed for 1,300 years is a considerable obstacle to social change. Marx once said that 'the critique of religion is the premise of all critique' (in an introduction to a critique of Hegel's philosophy of right), but some of his followers in the Arab world prefer not to start an ideological battle while fighting the political one. As for the critique of Islam in the Arab world – one can count on one hand the books written.[6] Even some left-wing organisations in Arab countries, like the Communist parties, often resort to the Koraan when justifying their activities to the masses. If we add to this the total subordination of women to men, and woman's image as an instrument for raising children or satisfying sexual needs, clannish loyalties, etc., we get an idea about some specific features influencing social and political struggles in this society.

The enormous wealth from oil revenues – a wealth unprecedented in history – is amassed by a handful of autocratic rulers whose authority is based on religion and the army, who are accountable to no political institutions representing the population. This is a glaring example of the influence of Western capitalism on Arab society, an influence strengthening the most conservative elements, and fighting (often with arms) against the progressive forces that aspire to democracy and equality. Another feature is the widespread popular desire to unify the Mashreq. Should this unification become a reality it will significantly change the balance of power in the area. Obviously the existing regimes, as well as the West, will obstruct such unification.

The Palestinians share all these features of Arab society compounded with the fact that for 27 years over a million of them have lived in refugee camps. The Palestinians have suffered loss of lands, homes and independence. Most share one common aim – to return to their lands and country and be a free people there. They will struggle against any political arrangement which ignores their political existence (for example, Resolution 242 of the UN) even if it is endorsed by other Arab regimes. Many Palestinians realise that the struggle against Zionism is not a struggle against the Jews. Many realise that three million Israelis will constitute a social and political problem even after the defeat of Zionism, and that they must be offered a political solution that is acceptable to a significant part of them. This approach suggests some possibilities:

1. an Arab Palestine next to an Israel on pre-1967 lines
2. a federal state
3. a single, joint, non-discriminatory state.

The first possibility implies a recognition of a Jewish state, that is, acceptance of a state discriminating against Palestinians. Even if some Palestinians were willing to accept this 'settlement' it would be rejected by many others. The revolutionary left should not support this arrangement which will contribute to the consolidation of ethnic barriers and enhance imperialist influence in the area.

The two other possibilities require as a prior stage the defeat of Zionism. Such a defeat would be significant and stable only if part of the Israeli population itself contributed to it. To succeed in this struggle it would not be enough to argue that Zionism had failed to fulfil its promises. One would have to show that even if it had succeeded it must be rejected, for it is a system depending for its identity on hostility and discrimination. The creation of a democratic, secular socialist state – whatever its borders – in which Jew and Arab can live together without discrimination is a positive aim to struggle for, and political principles must be chosen so as to further this aim rather than hinder it.

Realism and Vision in Revolutionary Politics

It is often argued that in the present circumstances of intense hostility the idea of a joint Jewish-Arab state is 'unrealistic', meaning that it cannot be achieved in the near future. Those who put forward this argument should first clarify whether they consider the idea to be desirable. By forcing the adversary to expose his desired aim an 'unrealistic' proposal can play a very realistic role. Moreover, the political realities of today were unrealistic visions a few decades ago. In politics the 'unrealistic' visionary is often the initiator of actions which culminate in the creation of a new reality. Revolutionary 'unrealistic' politics based on a vision of a desirable future have an essential role to play, they widen the horizons of imaginable possibilities and lend a direction to the political activity of the moment. Without such an 'unrealistic' aim politics is reduced to the 'art of achieving the possible'; with such an aim it is elevated to the 'art of achieving the desirable'.

Notes and References

1. First published in *On Target*, winter 1975/76, London.
2. Lenin, *Selected Works*, 1952, vol. 1, part 2, Moscow: State Publishing House, p. 319.
3. *Selected Works*, p. 360.
4. By 'state' we mean any political system.
5. *Selected Works*, p. 323.
6. Khaled El-Azem recently published *Critique of Religious Thought*, and was attacked by both the right and the left.

12

Socialism and the Nation-state[1]

The following essay is part of an ongoing debate within the Matzpen group in Israel on the issue of the 'democratic, secular, state in Palestine'. The author – who supports the idea of a democratic, secular, state, but proposes to develop it further along socialist lines, has added an introduction about the background to the debate.

Background

Most of the people who founded the Matzpen group in Israel in 1961 came from the Israeli Communist Party (ICP). They left the ICP because of political disagreements, one of which was the refusal of the ICP to see in Zionism the dominant motivation of Israeli policies. The Matzpen people insisted that Israel's policies were motivated by Zionist, rather than merely capitalist, interests, and that whenever these two came into conflict the capitalist interest was subordinated to the Zionist one. In short, that Israeli politics were dominated by Zionist considerations rather than by capitalist ones. This general disagreement on the basic nature of the Israeli state was linked to disagreements on actual, daily issues in Israel. Two of these were the ICP policy towards the *Histadrut* (the Zionist Labour corporation) and the ICP attitude to the Israeli policy towards those Palestinians who became citizens of Israel in 1948.

1. The *Histadrut* (the General Organisation of the Jewish Workers in the Land of Israel, founded in 1922) which refused to accept Arabs as members for 40 years, and conducted a 'Jewish labour only' campaign in the 1920s and 30s, was considered by the ICP to be 'a reactionary trade union'. Accordingly, the ICP pursued a traditional economistic policy in the Histadrut, aiming to gain a majority in internal elections and transform this corporation into a militant trade union. Matzpen people argued that the Histadrut was not merely a trade union but the largest proprietor and employer in the country (after the government), and that it was created – and served – as the economic power base of the Zionist labour movement. Such an organisation could not be 'reformed', even if the ICP won

an absolute majority in it; it had to be dismantled. The ICP refuses to this day to accept this assessment.

2. Israel's policy towards its Palestinian citizens was considered by the ICP as merely 'anti-democratic'. This policy – like the confiscation of lands, the restriction of freedom of movement and abode – was applied only to Palestinian citizens, never to Jews, indicating that 'anti-democracy' was applied on a selective basis. Newly arrived Jewish immigrants were settled in new Jewish towns (like Upper Nazareth, Karmiel, etc.) built in areas populated almost exclusively by Palestinians – who were forbidden to rent accommodation there. Everything pointed to the conclusion that Israeli policy towards its Palestinian citizens was the same as its policy towards the Palestinians generally, namely to dislodge them from their lands and present them with accomplished facts of Jewish settlement on their lands. This is not a new 'anti-democratic' policy invested in 1948 but the old Zionist policy from the start of the Zionist colonisation of Palestine. The ICP rejected this view. It considered 1948, when Israel was declared an independent state, as a turning point which made Zionism into a thing of the past and Israel into a reactionary bourgeois democracy. Matzpen argued that the state of Israel and its policies were a continuation of Zionism and not a qualitatively new phenomenon.

During the 1960s Matzpen was the only socialist, anti-Zionist organisation in Israel which saw in Zionism the source of the Israeli–Arab conflict. Since the 1967 war this view has become widely accepted. Matzpen challenged the official Israeli presentation of the Israeli–Arab conflict as 'irrational Arab hostility towards Jews' and put forward an analysis showing that the Palestinian Arabs were fighting for more than half a century against an exclusivist colonising movement depriving them of their lands and of their independence. As a result Matzpen was viciously attacked by the entire spectrum of Israeli political opinion. Despite disagreements there was one point on which Matzpen agreed with the ICP, namely that the Palestinian Arabs and the Israeli Jews each constitute a nation, and that their right to self-determination, including the right of each to create a nation-state of its own, must be recognised and honoured.

Matzpen – and the ICP – were opposed to nationalism as an ideology and to the nation-state as a political framework, but they argued that as long as the majority desired a nation-state this wish must be respected, that the abolition of the nation-state must be brought about by conviction, never by coercion.

This consideration gave rise to the tacit conclusion that the creation of two nation-states in Palestine, one for the Palestinian Arabs and one for the Israeli Jews is – under the given historical circumstances – in line with the struggle towards a socialist union of the whole region. This view was unchallenged in Matzpen until the idea of a 'secular, democratic Palestine' was put forward by the PLO.

When the PLO raised, in the early 1970s, the demand for a single, democratic secular state in Palestine (thereby rejecting the idea of two separate states) it created a new political climate. A single, non-discriminatory, political framework is a positive goal with which many people agree and which few will reject as undesirable. For the first time in the long history of the conflict in Palestine, the Palestinians put forward a political proposal which could not be treated by traditional political concepts and attitudes.

The PLO's proposal to create a single state in Palestine, that will not discriminate between 'Jew, Christian, and Muslim' implied that the PLO considered the Israeli Jews merely as a religious group, and not as a national entity. This caused some people in Matzpen to reject the entire PLO proposal, because Matzpen insisted that the Israeli Jews constitute a national, rather than religious, entity. These comrades in Matzpen argued that the PLO intended to create a Palestinian-Arab nation-state in Palestine in which Jews will have equal civil rights as individuals, but will not be granted the collective right to establish their own nation-state.

However, there is an alternative way to deal with this issue. If the PLO proposal is considered unsatisfactory it can be taken up and developed – rather than rejected – into a satisfactory proposal. If the PLO is willing to propose a state which does not discriminate by religion, one need not reject this by saying that the Israeli Jews are a nation and not a religious denomination. Instead, one can propose that this state should abolish national, as well as religious, discrimination, that it should not be a nation-state but a socialist, non-national, state. Even if the Israeli Jews insisted on having their own nation-state an Israeli socialist should struggle against it, on principled – rather than merely practical – grounds.

'But every nation has "the right" to create its nation-state', argued some comrades in Matzpen; 'No, the nation-state cannot be accepted as a collective right by socialists', answered others. The rejection of the nation-state as a collective 'right' by socialists was proposed by me in an article entitled 'State and Nationality in Palestine' (published in *On Target*, Winter 1975, and *Miftah*, 1976).[2] In reply to this article Matzpen published a statement (drafted by M. Machover) entitled 'A Summary of Our Position on the National Question'.[3] Machover's article, accepted by the majority in Matzpen as a group statement, criticised my article, and put forward the following arguments.

1. There is a qualitative difference between rights of individuals and rights of a collective group.
2. Creating a nation-state is a collective right.

3. Denial of this right constitutes national oppression.
4. Israeli Jews must not interfere in the manner Palestinian Arabs decide their collective future.
5. The principle of 'separation of ethnicity from state' confuses the collective rights (of a nation) with rights of the individual (e.g. on religious matters, as embodied in the principle of 'separation of religion from the state'). This confusion promotes national oppression.

These are the arguments which I discuss in the following pages.

Socialism and Value Systems

Every political creed is based on a value system. Socialism is no exception. It is based on the anthropocentric value system which asserts that all human beings (whatever the differences between them) have to be treated as equals and that the well-being of humanity as a whole takes precedence over the well-being of the individual or of collectivities. Accordingly socialism opposes all forms of discrimination by race, class, ethnicity, religion, sex, etc. Other value systems, like theocentrism, ethnocentrism, or egocentrism, have other dominant values. In the theocentric system humanity is subordinate to God, and the dominant value is God's will. Capitalism is an egocentric system. The well-being of the individual takes precedence over the well-being of the community, and even over that of humanity as a whole. Nationalism is a typical example of an ethnocentric value system. The well-being of an ethnic group (a tribe, clan, race, nation, etc.) takes precedence over the well-being of humanity, the individual, or God's will.

Within each value system there can be (and usually are) various interpretations of serving the dominant value, but whatever the particular interpretation the dominance of that value remains indisputable.

Conflicts between value systems are inevitable and occur between individuals or collectivities as well as within them. Whenever the inner conflicts become acute one is forced to resolve them by choosing one value system as dominant. In such cases it becomes clear that a compromise between two conflicting value systems is impossible. There are numerous examples to demonstrate this conclusion; the entire history of socialism is littered with examples of socialist movements and individuals who tried to reconcile socialism with nationalism yet were forced – in situations of conflict, like war – to choose between the two.

Many Zionists tried to merge Zionism with socialism, but whenever their Zionist activity in Palestine brought them into conflict with the Palestinians they had to choose between their conviction that 'all human beings must be treated as equals' and 'my nation right or wrong', that is, between Zionist ethnocentrism and socialist anthropocentrism, and most of them chose Zionism.

Another common conflict is that between a value system and the democratic principle of decision by majority. Here too one is often forced to choose; in most cases people will struggle against a majority decision which runs contrary to their dominant value. They will not grant such decision moral validity.

Each value system implies its ethics and moral code and shapes the behaviour and response of individuals and collectivities. Choices are prescribed by value systems, for individuals and collectivities alike. The well-being of the nation as a dominant value, and the nation-state as an inalienable right, are classic ethnocentric values. Anthropocentric socialism cannot accept these values. It may have to live with them but it cannot stop struggling against them. This struggle is one of principles, not practicalities. The struggle for socialism is about values, for the primacy of anthropocentrism over all other value systems. Hence a socialist cannot accept the moral legitimacy of the nation-state (cannot accept it as 'a right') even when the majority desires it. The same consideration applies with regards to tribal states, theocracies, or capitalist regimes. If socialism ceases to struggle for anthropocentrism it has relinquished its moral basis, and becomes ethno- or theo-centred.

Socialism and Collective Rights – What is a 'Right'?

A right is a demand which has been endowed with moral legitimacy. No one imputes moral legitimacy to every demand. To impute such legitimacy is a matter of accepting or rejecting a value system. This applies to individual and collective demands alike. For example, the moral legitimacy of killing people depends not only on the circumstances of this act but also upon the value system of those who interpret the act and the circumstances. Is a PLO raid into Israel an act of crime? Terror? Or war?

Collective demands are no different. A population may desire – and demand by majority vote – to establish a religious, tribal, or racial, political framework according to its theo- or ethno-centric value systems, to discriminate favourably of one particular religion, tribe or race, thereby discriminating against all others. No anthropocentric socialist can accept this mode of self-determination as 'a right'. Although a nation-state, tribal state or religious state is often brought into existence as a result of majority choice, and an anthropocentric socialist must take this into account and find meaningful ways of acting in such circumstances, this has nothing to do with the acceptance of, say, the religious state, as a 'right'. If the nation-state is accepted as a 'right' there is no principled reason for the struggle against it. What arguments can an anthropocentric socialist bring against the nation-state after accepting it as a morally legitimate political framework? Perhaps a few arguments about practicalities, that the nation-state is not a practical framework from a political and economic viewpoint, that it creates more difficulties than benefits. None of these is a principled argument rejecting the ethnocentric values of the nation-state. The champions of the nation-state will put forward a principled ethnocentric argument in favour of their system, insisting on the national interest, as the dominant criterion. If the socialist accepts the 'national interest' as the dominant criterion she/he subordinates anthropocentrism to ethnocentrism, and it is only a matter of time before she/he succumbs to ethnocentrism. But if the 'national interest' is rejected as a dominant value yet the nation-state is accepted as a 'right' the result is abdication from the ideological struggle against the nation-state. One then struggles against its consequences (ethnic wars, ethnic discrimination, etc.) but not against the political framework and value system which causes them.

There are socialists who regard the problem of morality in politics (and hence the entire problem of 'rights') as subordinated to the 'historical process'. This enables them to subordinate their own moral judgements to their conception of 'historical necessity'. Some even argue for the 'separation of morality from politics' and for accepting as 'moral' whatever they consider as 'historically necessary'. According to this argument the nation-state is a necessary historical phase and must therefore be accepted as a 'right' by socialists.

Those who uphold this view must answer three major questions:

1. what criteria determine whether a certain historical phenomenon is a 'historical necessity'? (for example, is Stalinism a 'historical necessity'?)
2. why are 'historical necessities' inherently moral? (for example, can slavery in antiquity, or capitalism today, be considered as moral, and the ownership of slaves, or exploitation of workers, be accepted as a 'right'?)
3. if politics are amoral why be political?

If the 'historical necessity' argument is allowed to dominate the value system it becomes difficult to reject the 'right of religions to political self-determination', and to oppose the religious state. Nowadays religion in Europe is – due to a long struggle in previous centuries – a personal issue, a matter of individual rights. But in the Islamic world – which has not yet passed through the historical phase of the struggle for separation of religion from the state – many still consider the religious state as their collective, rather than individual, right. In such a situation a fierce struggle has still to be fought to transform religion from a collective issue into a personal one. The Islamic world has its own historical process (despite all Western influence) and its own cultural and social dynamics, in which the Islamic republic may well be a 'historic necessity'. If the Islamic republic is a necessary phase in the historical evolution of Islamic civilisation, and if one considers 'historical necessities' as inherently moral, how can one reject the 'right of religions to political self-determination'?

Those socialists who reject this 'right' (although they may have to accept the fact) do so by judging historical phenomena (be they 'necessary' or 'unnecessary') according to the anthropocentric value system. And it is this struggle – and victory – of one value system over another, that transforms what has hitherto been considered as a 'collective right' into a right of the individual. A demand by a collectivity is not necessarily a 'right'. Only one's value system determines what is accepted as a 'right'.

Socialism and National Rights

Anthropocentric socialism has always been opposed to nationalism (and vice versa). The two value systems are irreconcilable. But the socialist movement has always been divided in its political answer to the 'national question'. The reason for this is simple: while all socialists are opposed to national oppression they do not all agree on the nation-state.

What acts and aspirations of a national collectivity should a socialist endorse as a 'right'?

Should this 'bill of national rights' include the nation-state? It was Lenin, in his article 'On the Right of Nations to Self-Determination', who stated: 'Self-determination of nations means the political separation of these nations from alien bodies, the formation of independent nation-states.'[4] It is this interpretation of national self-determination which is at the root of the entire controversy. Marx also dealt with the national question, and supported the struggles of the Poles and Irish for independence, but his support was based on the contribution of these struggles to the socialist revolution (weakening the Russian and British empires) and not on the 'right' to a nation-state. Rosa Luxemburg and Trotsky disagreed with Lenin on the national question, and Stalin published a long article ('Marxism and the National Question', 1913) to determine when a collectivity constitutes a 'nation' and merits the support of socialists in its struggle for its nation-state. Is this really necessary?

When people define themselves through their own prolonged and persistent struggle as a national collectivity (for example, the Palestinians, the Kurds, and the Israeli Jews) they will not abandon their struggle merely because someone else refuses to define them as a 'nation'. In history, collectivities are defined by their persistent struggle and not by formal definitions imposed by observers or opponents. The question therefore is not whether a certain collectivity constitutes a 'nation', but which demands of such a self-defined collectivity should an anthropocentric socialist accept as a 'right'.

Most socialists would agree that the use and development of the national language and culture should be recognised, and defended, as national 'rights'. But what about the nation-state, should it be accepted, by a socialist, as a 'right' too? Machover (and, at present, the majority in Matzpen) insist that the nation-state is a 'right'. Arguing against Dr Nabil Sha'ath's (PLO) view that the Israeli Jews be granted 'collective or group rights in addition to their individual rights ... the rights to develop as a group culturally and linguistically',[5] Machover asserts,

> We see, therefore, that both the famous explicit statement of the PLO formula, and its authorised interpretation, offer the Israeli Jews a future in which they will enjoy full equality of civil personal rights but will not be regarded as a national entity and so will not have real national rights.[6]

What are the 'real national rights' in addition to the collective right to free development of the language and culture?

> When a certain people aspires to establish a sovereign state of its own in the territory within which it constitutes a significant majority of the population, and this right is denied by the intervention of a foreign people – that also is national oppression, e.g. the Palestinians in Israel.[7]

This presentation of the problem is misleading. Every socialist will agree that external intervention by a foreign nation in the manner in which national self-determination is implemented constitutes an act of oppression. But this is not what the discussion is about. The discussion is about the attitude of socialists *within* each nation to the aspiration of others in that nation to create a nation-state.

Should an Israeli anthropocentric socialist accept the demand of most Israeli Jews to maintain their nation-state as a matter of 'right'? Should a democratic secular Palestine be rejected because it ignores the 'right' of the Israeli Jews to a state of their own? Yes! is the answer of Matzpen's statement, No! is my answer. 'No' to national oppression, and 'No' to the nation-state whose policies implement this oppression. *Ethnicity should be separated from the state just like religion.* We should struggle to overcome ethnic politics just as earlier generations of revolutionaries struggled to overcome religious politics. This will not be done by oppression nor by accepting the nation-state as a 'collective right'. On the contrary, the idea that the nation-state is a collective 'right' must be challenged. It is a demand which has to be considered, not a 'right' which has to be accepted. Anthropocentrism must confront ethnocentrism without making any concessions to its morality. Otherwise, if we accept the nation-state as a 'right', we are defeated before we started.

National Rights and National Oppression

The Matzpen statement lists three collective rights of a national collectivity:

1. the use of its own language and the development of its culture
2. political autonomy within a broader political framework
3. political sovereignty – a nation-state of its own.

The statement then asserts that the 'right of nations to self-determination' is the right to choose any of these three without external coercion or foreign intervention:

> In short, national oppression is primarily the denial of the right to self-determination. This itself being the fundamental national right, all other national rights are either included within it or follow from it, and, therefore, supporting the right to self-determination means neither more nor less than opposing national oppression. These are merely two forms of the same principle: one is formulated positively (support for the right ...), the other negatively (resistance to oppression ...). There is a tendency mainly for reasons of publicity and propaganda to prefer the positive form of expression, but that is a secondary consideration, a matter of formulation, and there is no difference of quality or principle between the two formulations.[8]

This assertion is false. We are not dealing with two formulations of one principle but with two different and conflicting principles. To illustrate this let us consider a religious, racial or tribal collectivity which rejects the notion of separation of religion, race or tribe from the state, and considers these matters to be collective rather than personal issues. If such a collectivity is discriminated against, and oppressed, on religious, racial or tribal grounds it is the duty of every socialist to oppose this oppression and struggle for its abolition. When this oppression – be it by one's 'own' rulers or by foreign force – is overthrown the oppressed differ among themselves as to the shape of their political future. There will be proposals to establish a religious, racial or tribal state which may have majority support by those who were oppressed on these grounds. Must a socialist – a member of that population – support a religious, racial or tribal state?

Certainly not! Is this opposition to the 'right of religions, races or tribes to political self-determination' equivalent to religious, racial or tribal oppression? Certainly not! To struggle against national oppression is one thing, to accept the nation-state as a 'right' is a totally different matter. Machover's formulation about 'external' coercion or 'foreign' intervention evades the issue. Of course 'foreigners' should not coerce the collectivity, but according to what criterion should the 'insiders' choose and act? According to what principle would Machover struggle against the wish of the majority of the Israeli Jews to maintain a nation-state of their own in Palestine? If the Israeli Jews wish to implement what Machover considers as their 'right', on what grounds can he struggle against it?

National collectivities exist and have collective rights (to use and develop their language and culture, run their own cultural and communal affairs, etc.) but must a socialist include the nation-state in the ' Bill of National Rights'? Can a socialist reject the nation-state morally but accept it politically? Can the problem be avoided by saying that 'we' must not interfere in the manner in which 'they' exercise their political rights? What principle should guide 'us' when we struggle against 'our' nationalists who insist on maintaining 'our' nation-state?

Machover insists that no other principle is necessary:

> The principle of the right to self determination, ie of resistance of all forms of national oppression, is the only general principle we, as socialists, have for the national question. We have no special ideal or detailed model which we wish to implement in every case. Nationality is not, for us, of value in its own right, and is certainly not a supreme value. Our position is determined in each given case according to the interests of the struggle for Socialism. Therefore, we do not need, nor can we accept, any additional general principles on the national question.[9]

This emphatic assertion – directed against the principle of 'separation of ethnicity from the state' – evades the central issue, namely: what is the basic socialist solution to the problem of relation between nation and state? No one is asking for 'special' ideals or 'detailed' models, but if there is no guiding principle to uphold a non-ethnic political system, while there is an acceptance of the nation-state as a 'right', then socialism suffers from a glaring inability to confront the problem of relations between nation and state. Moreover, a socialist who accepts the nation-state as one of the national rights is certainly not free to decide 'in each case, according to the interests of the struggle for socialism'. If the majority opts for a nation-state such a socialist must endorse this choice as a 'right' even if it obstructs the struggle for socialism. The entire history of the Communist Party in Palestine is an example of socialists opposed to the nation-state, fully aware that a Jewish nation-state in Palestine constitutes a major obstacle to the struggle for socialism in the Mashreq, but supporting it all the same because of their acceptance of the 'right' of nations to self-determination. Only when the nation-state is not considered a 'right' is one free to oppose (or support) it according to the interests of the struggle for socialism. When it is accepted as a 'right' this freedom is lost. Machover's formulation implies a situation wherein a national collectivity struggles to create a nation-state and a socialist – who considers this particular state as an obstacle to the struggle for socialism – says to this collectivity: 'I recognise your right to establish a nation-state, but since it obstructs the struggle for socialism I am against your implementation of that right.' No one can take such an argument seriously. Either one accepts the nation-state as a 'right' thereby relinquishing the freedom to judge each given case according to the interests of socialism, or one judges each struggle for a nation-state according to the interests of socialism, and then one cannot accept the nation-state as a matter of 'rights'. 'The interests of the struggle for socialism' and 'the right to create a nation-state' are two different principles which can – and often do – come into conflict, requiring that one be relinquished, but which one? Nothing in the Matzpen statement suggests that in such conflict the principle of the 'right to a nation state' should be rejected. On the contrary, the style of the formulations hints that under no circumstances will Matzpen deal seriously with the criticism of its traditional position on the national question, or reconsider its rejection of the Palestinian proposal for a democratic, secular Palestine. This is to be regretted because whatever the drawbacks of this proposal it is certainly more in line with the interests of a socialist unification of the entire Mashreq than is the alternative one of two separate nation-states in Palestine. It can form the basis of dialogue between Jewish and Arab socialists in Palestine on the structure of one, non-nationalistic and non-sectarian, common socialist state, as a common goal for a common struggle. The 'two nation-states' alternative can provide none of these positive possibilities. It is really remarkable that after more than half a century of struggle against the Zionist colonisation in Palestine the Palestinian resistance movement could come up with a proposal to create a common political framework that would treat the Israeli Jew as an equal cultural collectivity, and that the Palestinians should do so while still being oppressed by those to whom they make this offer. The magnanimity of this offer deserves that it be taken up and developed – especially by the anti-Zionist left in Israel, rather than be dismissed curtly because it 'does not recognise the existence of a Hebrew (Israeli-Jewish) nation and hence does not grant this collectivity any national rights'.

The Historical Decline of National Rights

> If, and when, the socialist vision of the disappearance of all
> national barriers comes true, then the concept of the nation will
> lose its basis in reality, and thereby will national rights lose their
> meaning. In this article, however, we do not discuss the historical
> dimension of nationalism and the national question only the form
> in which it exists in our time.[10]

'If, and when, the socialist vision of the disappearance of all national
barriers comes true ...' but not a word on *how* it will come true.
Will the socialist vision come true due to some abstract 'historical
process' or does it require the active struggle of socialists to make
it come true? To make this vision come true in the future there must
be an active struggle for it today. This struggle must have two
qualities: it must challenge the existing political system and it must
propose an alternative political system for replacing the existing one.
This applies to national barriers too. One must challenge the
nation-state and propose an alternative political system. 'Down with
national oppression' and 'down with the nation-state' is only the
negation of the existing state of affairs. 'For a non-ethnic, socialist
state which separates ethnicity from the state' is the positive alternative. The nation-state will not 'lose' its meaning and give rise to
some hazy socialist alternative in the distant future without a
socialist struggle to create this alternative. It is unrealistic and
wrong to say: right now nationalism is an actual reality so let us
endorse the nation-state as a 'right', hoping that later, when the
socialist vision comes true, the nation-state will disappear of its own.
If anthropocentrists do not struggle against ethnocentrism it will
not disappear. If anthropocentrists grant moral legitimacy to the
nation-state they abdicate from the struggle against it.

> The right to self-determination includes the right to establish
> a separate nation-state. However a right is not a duty, and
> therefore we do not commit ourselves to encourage, in each and
> every case, the creation of a separate nation-state, but we
> commit ourselves at least to accept the creation of such a state
> if it can only be prevented by coercion and national oppression.[11]

A 'right' is not a duty, but it confers legitimacy. If we accept the
nation-state as a 'right', how can we oppose it in the absence of
coercion? Coercion is certainly not the way to combat ethnocentric values and their political expression in the nation-state, but how
can socialists who accept this state as a 'right' convince anyone that
it should be rejected? By endorsing the nation-state morally one
destroys the moral basis of the struggle against it.

There is another argument against the anthropocentric principle
of 'separation of ethnicity from the state', which, though rarely stated

explicitly, acts as a powerful motivation, namely: that those who promote this principle within a generally nationalistic minded society will become totally isolated from the broad masses of the population, and will thereby forfeit any chance of becoming a political force in their society. This may indeed be the case. But it can only serve as a valid argument for those who conceive of revolution primarily in political terms.

Is revolution concerned primarily with the change of political authority relations, or with the change of the value system?

All the revolutions in this century concerned themselves primarily with achieving political power. But even where political revolutionaries accepted the idea that political power was not an end in itself but a means to assist in the change of the value system, they found themselves imprisoned by the old value system. We find, after seven decades of political revolutionary struggles and victories, that too many of the values of the previous regimes persist in the post-revolutionary regime. In other words, revolutionaries who did not challenge the value system which dominated the old regime found themselves prisoners of that value system in the new regime which they created. The political system changed, but the value system remained.

This indicates a basic flaw in a revolutionary activity concerned primarily with power politics. There is an urgent need to broaden the domain of revolutionary activity so as to include an active struggle to promote a new value system centred not on the nation, tribe, class or individual, but on humanity as a whole. The struggle to promote this value system against rival value systems has to take place alongside the struggle to change political power, and must not be postponed until 'after the revolution'. Once this idea is accepted the struggle to 'separate state from nation, religion, race or class' becomes an integral part of the revolutionary struggle rather than an additional obstacle. In any case, there is an element of choice in this dilemma, and those revolutionaries who choose to concentrate their activity on power politics can only blame their own decision if they find themselves in their new regime dominated by the values of the old regime. On the other hand, if the struggle for the new values is recognised as fundamental there is no reason why it should not start here and now.

Notes and References

1. First published in Asmar, F., Davis, U. and Khadr, N., *Towards a Socialist Republic of Palestine*, 1978, London: Ithaca Press.
2. Reprinted in *Debate on Palestine*, 1981, London: Ithaca Press.
3. Matzpen (drafted by M. Machover), 'A Summary of Our Position on the National Question', *Red Pages*, no. 4, 1978.

4. *Selected Works*, 1952, vol. 1, part 2, Moscow: State Publishing House, p. 319.
5. Nabil Sha'ath, *Towards Democratic Palestine*, English edition, 19 January 1970.
6. *A Summary*, p. 32
7. *A Summary*, p. 32
8. *A Summary*, p. 33.
9. *A Summary*, pp. 33, 34.
10. *A Summary*, p. 33.
11. *A Summary*, p. 36.

13

Who is Afraid of Satan?[1]

Many of those struggling to overcome the abject conditions of people in the third world have come to realise that their efforts are often frustrated by institutionalised belief systems there. Birth control is a good example – certain systems of belief hinder its use even when individuals and governments agree that it could greatly improve living standards. In a country like Egypt, where the population increases by a million every eight months, the development of housing, health and education facilities is unable to keep pace.

Individuals and governments alike find themselves shackled by beliefs and traditions shaped centuries ago and totally out of touch with the modern world. This applies to Catholicism, Orthodox Judaism, Islam, and many other beliefs held by various tribes and religious populations. People brought up in the West tend to underestimate the strong involvement of some religions with politics.

In the West the battle for the separation of religion from politics and from the state has been won. Nearly all Western believers accept that religious beliefs are a personal affair and must not be imposed by law upon others. By contrast, Islam is a religion concerned with establishing a religious community. It is a political religion, concerned with society as much as with the individual. It opposes the principle of separation of religion from politics. It has strong views on global politics. It struggles to ensure that religious law becomes and remains state law, and aspires to conduct domestic and foreign policy according to religious principles. Most Westerners are unaware of the fact that the difficult struggle to separate religion from politics has yet to be won in many Islamic societies.

Even before the *Satanic Verses* affair many Muslims felt under attack by Western cultural values. This may come as a surprise to most Westerners. They fail to appreciate that the spread of Western culture and values (by means of Western technology) constitutes a threat to other cultures. Islam is not just a religious belief, it is the cultural core of many societies. It provides group identity and moral guidance. People in the third world fear that the impact of the West will cause them to lose their group identity. Some worry about the erosion of their code of morality. Western attitudes towards women and sex are particularly offensive to many Muslims. Islam upholds a view of society – and Paradise – where the male is dominant. This applies to sex, law, economics and family life. Sexual contact between people who are not married is considered a sin – it is a serious offence for a man (even more so for a woman), often punished by death. Women's sexual pleasure is a taboo subject. Women's liberation may well be the most explosive social issue in Islamic countries.

Family honour is a dominant value in Islamic societies. Its burden is carried mainly by the woman. A philandering man will be forgiven, because his act is not considered a serious stain on the honourable reputation of his family, but a woman's extramarital sex is considered intolerable, shaming her entire family, and is unforgiveable. Even a raped woman is considered a stain on the family honour. As Islam upholds these notions anything which challenges them constitutes a threat to the faith. Any view which tolerates extramarital sex (and fails to see it as a moral or legal offence) is considered 'corrupt', 'immoral', and an attack on the one and only 'righteous' attitude, hence the feeling of many Muslims that 'the Crusades are not over'. They still feel under attack from Christianity.

The third world is keen to acquire Western technology but it is totally unaware of the fact that in doing so it imports a cultural Trojan horse. The maintenance of modern technology on a social scale requires widespread technological and scientific education which is inextricably linked to philosophical principles. These principles are incompatible with religious dogmas. For example, the principle of testing a theory (or a belief) by means of repeatable experiments is bound to downgrade beliefs which can never be tested by experiment.

Islamic civilisation is defending itself against the impact of Western civilisation. It feels (and is) under attack, even though the West is mounting no conscious attack on Islamic beliefs and has no intention of doing so. It is the inventions of the West (which the Islamic world so desires) that constitute the cultural threat. A society which desires the fruits of Western civilisation cannot ignore the philosophical seeds. These seeds radiate a different set of principles, values and beliefs. The Amish sect in the USA knew this and decided to isolate itself completely from all modern technology. A sect can do so, but a state cannot, particularly when it faces the possibility of armed conflict with another state. It is not merely TV, radio, aeroplanes and rockets which undermine traditional theistic beliefs; every product of science used on a social scale is a cultural agent contributing to the breakdown of traditional beliefs. All traditional cultures, beliefs and morals – including those of the West itself – are undermined by modern technology.

Some of the responses of Iran's clergy to the legalistic attitude of Western governments in the *Satanic Verses* affair display symptoms of paranoia. Those in authority in Iran cannot grasp that no Western government can remain indifferent to a public incitement by the leading figure in a foreign country to assassinate one of its citizens or to burn bookshops selling a particular book. These people genuinely believe that there is a planned, co-ordinated, and well-organised conspiracy by Western powers against Islam, and that Salman Rushdie's book is part of it.

Western analysts, on the other hand, are blinkered by their belief that religious and cultural anxieties are a mere pretext whereas 'power politics' are the 'real' issue. They interpret Islamic responses exclusively as manipulative moves in the political power game in the Islamic world. This too is a 'plot theory'. Each side interprets the other's motives according to its own. The possibility that the other side could have a genuinely different notion of existence threatens them with the relativisation of their own notion.

There is an undeniable spiritual crisis in most societies today. The effort to cling to traditional beliefs is one of its manifestations. The aggressive response of some beliefs is, in historical terms, a defensive move. An attempt to hang on to certainties which have served for many years is only to be expected. Though understandable, it is a useless effort. The inventions of modern science create actual social conditions (and confront humanity with problems) which have never existed before. Any belief system (including secular ones) which fails to adapt to new conditions becomes irrelevant to people who live under these conditions. Adaptation means change, and change generates an ongoing crisis of belief. Failure to adapt means isolation, stagnation and irrelevance. Groups who can't, or won't, change, end as sects.

The examples of the North and South American Indians, the Japanese, the Jews, the African tribal cultures, and the Eskimos, all indicate that there are only two alternatives for traditional cultures in the modern world: isolation or assimilation. Any other way is a palliative, postponing the inevitable choice. All attempts to establish states based on traditional laws in the contemporary world are doomed. They are defensive attempts to preserve identities which are losing their validity, and merely prolong the process of assimilation by a few decades. They often force the traditional cultures to adopt measures which discredit them in the eyes of their own adherents. Moreover, internal schisms within regimes based on traditional cultures are inevitable, adding confusion to loss of credibility. These difficulties are compounded by the fact that, unlike a century ago, the West today cannot offer any meaningful substitute for beliefs which have become untenable. There is a spiritual void at the centre of Western civilisation. Moreover, Western philosophy, too, and even the philosophical foundations of theoretical science, are themselves in a crisis. It is not an attractive situation for many Westerners either. But adherence to unconvincing beliefs is an act of self-deception which is even less attractive.

Islam was, originally, progressive in comparison with other creeds prevailing in Arabia at the time of its foundation. It is still concerned more than other creeds with the life of the community rather than the individual. It aspires to create a community based on social justice. One of the religious duties of the believer is the relief of the poor. However, it has never undergone a reformation, nor was there an ideological movement that offered a critique of Islam. Little has changed in Islam since the days of Mohammed. Given the current crisis of Western culture (which has ceased to inspire, spiritually, many of its own members) one can sympathise with the plight of Muslims who see their own culture undermined without any positive alternative to replace it.

Ayatollah Khomeini's victory in Iran and the declaration of an Islamic republic came as a total surprise to most Westerners, including academic specialists in the USA, USSR and Europe. A few have become wise after the event. Most have not. Marxists in particular (including Iranian Marxists) grossly underestimated Islam's political significance. They forgot Marx's observation that the critique of religion is the starting point of all social critique. They avoided a confrontation in the cultural domain, and devoted themselves to economic and political issues, refraining from making a critique of Islam for fear of antagonising the mass of the population.

Most Marxists' thinking was – and still is – dominated by economic and political categories. They considered the cultural and spiritual issues as marginal elements of 'the superstructure'. But the Islamic leadership addressed itself to the cultural anxieties of the population, to its fear of losing identity, to its rejection of Western culture and morality. The cultural campaign of Islam for preservation of traditional identity and morality was not challenged by the left. It was challenged by the Shah. When the Shah was defeated it was also the defeat of the Western values he had tried to impose. The victory of Khomeini meant that all atheist ideologies like socialism or Marxism became targets for destruction. The subsequent massacre of the left in Iran was a foregone conclusion.

It is of the utmost urgency for the left in Islamic societies to provide a historical interpretation of Islam. This task is forced upon them by the ideological resurgence of Islam. In the absence of a historical interpretation of religion people will accept a religious interpretation of history. There can be no vacuum in this domain, even when people are unaware of the fact that they accept – implicitly – one interpretation or another. When matters come to a head this metaphysical controversy is settled by the sword (as some Muslims openly declare). Many Iranian Marxists discovered this truth too late in front of the religious firing squads.

Modern science undermines all traditional religions. No wonder that many believers feel fragile and defensive. However, some beliefs are more fragile than others. The fragility of Islam is demonstrated by the response to Rushdie's book. The vehement public outrage of many believers, especially the threats of physical violence, requires some analysis. A belief which needs laws, threats or violence to protect it from criticism, doubt or ridicule is insecure and weak. Resorting to authority, loyalty, coercion or punishment (in defence of any belief) reveals weakness, not strength. This applies to any creed, philosophy or dogma, including secular ones. Stalin's decision to kill Trotsky revealed his inability to produce ideas to counter Trotsky's. If you feel threatened by an idea and cannot defend yourself by a counter idea you may try to eliminate the author or the book, but it never works. An idea can only be defeated by another idea. Killing an author or banning books amounts in the long run to self-defamation. Bookburning has been practised by many religions and regimes; it never did away with an idea, and it degraded its perpetrators. When Trotsky was finally assassinated on Stalin's orders, it seemed – to shortsighted observers – as if Stalin had won. One need not be a prophet (or a Trotskyist) to know that when the facts in the Stalin/Trotsky controversy are fully revealed Stalin will turn out to be the villain and Trotsky the martyr.

The spiritual strength of a belief depends on the conviction of the believers. If this conviction is based on fear or anxiety, on conditioning, loyalty of any kind, submission to any authority, or on suspension of one's own criticisms, then the believer will be very vulnerable to criticism or ridicule. There is an inherent weakness in any belief based on such considerations, and no threats against blasphemers can strengthen it. God is not upset by blasphemy – believers are. Believers who are outraged by blasphemy are defending themselves, not their God.

Conversely, if the belief is the result not of conditioning, fear or loyalty, but of inner, positive conviction, it will not be threatened by ridicule or blasphemy. It will not need laws, punishment or violence against blasphemers, critics or reformers. The ancient Greeks and Romans already knew that an outraged response only revealed one's own weakness: 'You are angry, Jupiter, hence you must be wrong.'

The Islamic responses to Rushdie's book created a new situation. It is no longer possible to keep silent about Islam. Socialists and atheist nationalists in Islamic societies have mostly held back from a cultural critique of religion. The *Satanic Verses* affair makes a continuation of this stance untenable. Islam has declared a cultural war on atheism. Atheist silence on Islam implies surrender and a step down the road to religious executions. It is now imperative to start a campaign of cultural critique of religion within Islamic societies.

A cultural critique of religion does not imply distortion, ridicule or abuse. What is required is a historical interpretation of the belief and of its origins, an accurate account of its main features and of its crises within its historical context, an analysis of its dogma, texts and internal contradictions. It requires factual information about its founders, based on archaeological and textual research. It requires a social and psychological analysis of its moral code, sexual attitudes, fantasies of Paradise, taboos and notions of sin and of evil. Finally, it requires studies of similarities with and differences from other faiths. Actualisation must replace deification and demonisation.

A cultural critique never produces immediate results. It takes a generation or two before its effects are felt. But if one fails to make a start one cannot expect results. Since Islam is not particularly tolerant towards its critics (especially those from within its own ranks) it takes a lot of courage to produce a critique. No wonder critics are so few. But what alternative is there?

Salman Rushdie rendered Islamic civilisation a historical service. Whether he intended it or not, he has started a process, a cultural controversy which – like a nuclear chain-reaction – cannot be stopped. This process, long overdue, required a suitable historical situation and a sensitive, knowledgeable, courageous insider to start it going. It cannot be stopped now. Rushdie's assassination would only make things worse for Islam. Islam is stained by the threat against Rushdie; if the threat is carried out Islam will be stained in the eyes of most people on this planet, including many Muslims. The internal conflicts within Islam will reach an unprecedented pitch. Needless to say, all future Islamic incantations about the compassion and mercifulness of Allah will sound like one of Satan's jokes. If Islam needs to defend itself let it do so positively, by attracting people to its advantages, not by scaring them, by winning over the minds of its critics, not by assassinating them.

The left in Islamic societies is, unfortunately, wary of starting a cultural confrontation with Islam. Initiating a critique (in addition to the political struggles against reactionary rulers) is extremely difficult. The trouble is that the left has also considered such a task irrelevant. The Iranian left has paid with its life for its silence on the religious issue during the Shah's time. Many argued that religion was a marginal issue, others that it was tactically wrong to start a cultural struggle against enemies of the Shah. Tactically this made sense at the time; but can one now ignore the full consequences demonstrated by the Iranian experience?

Those who believe in the existence of Allah must also believe in the existence of Satan. Who is afraid of Satan? Only those who believe in him. If – according to their belief – Satan exists and is so powerful, how can they be sure that the voice which tells them to fight him is not his own? Those who do not share this belief ought to follow Rushdie. They should publicise their own view about Satan, about those who believe in his existence, and about the origins and consequences of the belief itself. They may not avoid the fire beyond death, but they may, perhaps, avoid this side of it.

Note

1. First published in *Solidarity* (London), vol. 21, autumn 1989.

14

1993 – Palestine: Occupied Territory To Become a Bantustan

The mutual recognition of the Palestine Liberation Organisation headed by Yasser Arafat and the Israeli government headed by Mr Rabin, culminating in their handshake on the White House lawn on 13 September 1993 marks a turning point in a century-long conflict between immigrant Zionist settlers and the indigenous Arab population of Palestine. It was inevitable that the Zionist organisation, founded in 1897 in Basle, Switzerland, with the aim of creating in Palestine a state for the Jews would come into conflict with the native Palestine Arabs who had their own aspirations for independence.

In 1918 Palestinian Arabs, living in a dozen cities and hundreds of villages, outnumbered Palestine Jews by ten to one. The few Jews in Palestine, mostly religious people who lived peacefully with the Arabs, opposed secular Zionism; they insisted that political redemption must be preceded by religious redemption and could only be brought about by God.

The Zionist organisation, founded in Europe by atheist Jews wishing to assimilate into the modern world, was the Jewish version of secular European nationalism. Zionism institutionalised a major schism in the Jewish civilisation, between secular nationalists and the religious Jews. It introduced an ethnocentric value system into a civilisation founded on theocentrism. It capitalised on the *de facto* divide between religious and non-religious Jews and established an organisation that aimed to create an ethnocentric state for Jews. Most founders of Zionism tried at first to assimilate as individuals into their host societies. Only after encountering social discrimination did some of them decide to form an organisation for creating a nation-state for Jews. Their goal: to enable Jews to assimilate as a group rather than as individuals. As they were prevented from becoming 'a person like all other persons', they decided to try to become 'a nation like all other nations'. Since Zionism aimed to create a state it became known as 'political Zionism'. Its founder, the assimilationist Vienna journalist Theodore Herzl, was ready to found that state anywhere. His followers insisted that the state be founded only in Palestine (whose biblical name 'Zion' gave the organisation its name).

The Zionists, a small minority among Jews, established a national council in Europe, an executive committee, a secretariat, a treasury, president, deputy president, propagandists and activists, to promote Jewish immigration to Palestine. They raised funds and organised immigration to Palestine. Zionist foreign policy was formulated by Max Nordau, the famous French author, in the second Zionist Congress as follows: 'Our aspirations lie in Palestine therefore our foreign policy must always be orientated towards that world power whose sphere of influence includes Palestine.' Accordingly, the Zionist organisation tried to prove its usefulness first to the Ottoman rulers and to their German allies. Later, when Britain won the First World War, Zionism shifted towards the USA which became, after the Suez War in 1956, the dominant world power in the region. Until the creation of Israel in 1948 no immigrant could enter Palestine without a permit from its rulers. The Zionist organisation had to prove to the British that Jewish immigration to Palestine could serve their interests. It did so by helping the British defeat the Palestinian peasant rebellion which lasted from 1936 to 1939. Zionists manned the ports and railways which were paralysed by the six-month general strike of the Palestinians. They also volunteered to the armed police.

The goal of a Jewish nation-state in Palestine, and the necessity to collaborate with the foreign rulers of Palestine, forced the Zionist movement into an inevitable conflict with the Arabs there. The Palestinians wanted independence; the Zionists opposed this. They wanted to turn Palestine into their state. The Palestinians demanded that the British rulers curb Jewish immigration to Palestine; the Zionists opposed this. They wanted to increase the number of Jews in Palestine and to outnumber the Arabs there in order to claim independence for themselves.

The Jewish thinker Asher Ginzburg foresaw this inevitable conflict. He visited Palestine in 1881 and under the pen-name of Ahad-Ha'am ('one of the people') reported on the situation of the settlements which the (non-Zionist) French Jewish Baron Edmund de Rothschild founded there before political Zionism came into being. In his article 'Truth from Palestine' (1891), Ahad-Ha'am stated:

> We are used to believe abroad that Palestine nowadays is entirely desolate, a desert without vegetation, and that anyone desiring to buy land there can come and buy to his heart's content. This is really not the case. Throughout the land it is hard to find arable land that is not cultivated. Only sandy areas or rocky mountains which are suitable only for planting trees, and this too after much

labour and great expense, are not cultivated because the Arabs are unwilling to work hard in the present for the sake of a distant future. Therefore not every day can one find good land for sale. Not only the [Palestinian] peasants but also the big [Palestinian] landowners will not easily sell good land which has no blemishes. Many of our [Jewish] brethren who came to buy land spent months in the country, toured it all over, yet failed to find what they were looking for. We are used to believe abroad that the Arabs are all savages from the desert, ignorant like animals, who neither see nor understand what happens around them. This is a great mistake. The Arab, like all Semites, has a sharp mind and is very cunning. All the towns of Syria and Palestine are full of Arab traders who know how to exploit the masses and how to outsmart their customers. Just like in Europe. The Arabs, particularly those who live in the towns, see and understand our aims and activities in Palestine. They pretend not to know because they see no threat to their future in what we do and they try to exploit us too, and make use of the newcomers as best they can, while laughing at us in their heart. The peasants rejoice when a Jewish colony is established because they get good wages for their labour there and enrich themselves every year. The big landowners are glad too because we pay for sandy and stony soil a high price they never dreamt about in the past.

However should a time come when the life of our people in Palestine will develop to such an extent as to push out, to a small or large extent, the indigenous population of the country, then not easily will they give up their place.[1]

This report, the result of a scrupulous inspection of Baron Rothschild's colonies in Palestine, was published six years before Herzl founded political Zionism in Switzerland. It gives the lie to the Zionist slogan that Palestine was 'a land without people' which ought to be given to the Jewish 'people without a land'. Ahad-ha'am foresaw the conflict between Zionist immigrants and Palestinian people long before it started. This was not a prophecy or some brilliant insight but an unbiased evaluation of the facts. Most political Zionists were unable to give an unbiased opinion when discussing Palestine. Ahad-Ha'am was a 'cultural Zionist' not a political one. He was critical of political Zionism. He even foresaw the alliance between the Zionist state and any imperial power dominating the Middle East. In 1898, a year after Herzl founded political Zionism, Ahad-Ha'am criticised the entire concept of political Zionism in an article entitled 'Political Zionism – The Jewish State and the Jewish Problem'. In this article he argued that the so-called 'Jewish problem' was, when viewed from the perspective of Jewish history, not a problem of persecution but a problem of loss of Jewish cultural identity due to secularisation. He argued that the loss of cultural identity could not be cured by the creation of a state.

Herzl's assimilationist state could not produce a Jewish culture because Herzl and his followers, being assimilationists aspiring 'to be like all other people', lacked any idea of the specific cultural features of the historical Jewish people. Ahad-Ha'am states in this article:

> The secret enabling our nation to survive is, as I have shown elsewhere, that already in antiquity its prophets taught it to respect only spiritual power and never to admire physical power. Therefore it has not succumbed, like all ancient people, to a loss of identity when facing stronger adversaries. As long as it upholds this principle it has a solid foundation in life since as a spiritual power it is not inferior to other nations and has no reason for loosing its identity. However a political idea alien to this national culture can turn the people's heart away from spiritual power and produce a tendency to seek its 'honour' by achieving physical power and political independence, thus severing the thread linking it with its past and losing the base which sustained it throughout history. Needless to add that should this [Zionist] enterprise fail, the result will be very sad for the nation will loose both spiritually and physically. Yet even if this enterprise succeeds, given our present moral state, when not only the nation, but also its spirit is dispersed and divided, Judaism will be in grave danger. All our leaders, whose education and status enable them to stand at the head of the state, are far from Judaism in spirit and have no idea of its strength and value. Such people, even if loyal to the state and wishing it success, will, necessarily, seek this success in terms of the alien culture which they have absorbed. They will implant this culture by moral influence and even by force in that State. So that the state of the Jews will finally be a state like that of the Germans, or French, only inhabited by Jews. A small example of this process exists already now [1898] in Palestine. History teaches that during Herod's kingdom Israel was indeed the 'State of the Jews' but the Jewish culture was rejected and persecuted. The monarchy wasted the nation's resources to build circuses and temples for idols. Such a state of the Jews will be mortal poison to our people and will grind its spirit in the dust. It will not become a physical power and it will not know its spiritual power. This small state, which will be like a playing ball in the hands of its neighbours, will survive only by diplomatic intrigues and by constant servility to the powers that happen to be dominant, it will fail to fill the

nation's spirit with pride, and the national culture, which could fill it with pride, has not been implanted in it and is alien to it. Thus it will really be, much more than now, 'a small, miserable, people', a spiritual slave to whoever happens to be dominant looking enviously and greedily at the fist of its mighty neighbours, and all its existence as a 'state owner' will not add an honourable chapter in its history. Isn't it preferable for 'an ancient people, which has been a light unto nations', to disappear from history rather that reach such a final goal? (p. 138)

This devastating critique of political zionism is totally unknown to Jews in Israel and abroad today. Ahad-Ha'am has been marginalised, and his works are known only to a few. However, in his day he was the foremost secular Jewish thinker, mentor of the national poet Bialik, and of Haim Weizman, leader of Zionism after Herzl and Israel's first President. Although 'The Jewish State and the Jewish Problem' deals primarily with the problem of secular Jewish identity, it contains a prognosis of Zionist foreign policy which has been confirmed by a century of Zionist, and later Israeli, politics.

Ahad-Ha'am foresaw the inevitability of a conflict between the Zionist project and the Palestinian Arabs. Zionist colonisation of Palestine differed from other European colonisations of countries in Africa in the nineteenth century. Most Zionist settlers did not venture on private colonisation enterprises. They were financially assisted, and politically supported, by the Zionist organisation. They fitted into an overall plan designed to turn Palestine into a state of the Jews, though Jews were a small minority in it. After the First World War, when the Zionist labour movement became the dominant force within political Zionism, it started a campaign to pressurise Jewish employers in Palestine to employ Jews only and to sack Arab workers. This exacerbated the conflict even more. No wonder that already in the early 1920s the Palestinian Arabs began to struggle against the British rulers and Zionist immigration. They conducted an ongoing struggle for independence which culminated in a three-year uprising against the British (1936–1939). This conflict erupted again after 1967, and particularly after 1987.

During this long conflict there were occasions when an agreement could have been reached between the warring sides. The most important were in 1948, 1956 and 1967. In 1948 Israel became an independent state by virtue of the United Nations resolution of 29 November 1947, which divided Palestine into two parts and decreed a Jewish state in one part and a Palestinian state in the other. This plan was rejected by the Arab world which denied the right of the UN to partition a territory inhabited for 1,300 years by Arabs. Britain, having lost part of its empire by this resolution, decided to employ its influence in Iraq, Egypt and Trans-Jordan, and organised an invasion of regular Arab armies into Palestine, intending to force the UN to ask it to resume British rule in Palestine until the 'restless natives' were 'mature' for independence.

Contrary to British expectations, the Israeli Jews managed to defeat the Egyptian, Syrian and Iraqi armies and achieved their coveted statehood. However, during the 1948 war the leader of Israel, David Ben-Gurion, negotiated a secret deal with King Abdallah of Trans-Jordan. The gist of the deal was that the territory which the UN allocated to the Palestinian state would be carved up and divided between Israel and Trans-Jordan. Each would annex about half the territory and in return King Abdallah would not join the Arab war against Israel. This deal was carried out. As a result Israel increased its territory while the Palestinians were left with nothing. By taking part in this deal Ben-Gurion violated the UN partition resolution and lost the international recognition for Israel's borders as prescribed by the UN. By annexing territories allocated by the UN to the Palestinians, Ben-Gurion created new borders unrecognised by the international community.

Had Ben-Gurion stayed within the borders of the UN partition plan, then any Arab grievance about Palestine would have had to be addressed to the UN. Israel could argue, rightly, that it had merely obeyed a decision taken by the international community. The Palestinian Arabs would have had to conduct their struggle for independence against King Abdallah and could blame Trans-Jordan, or the UN, rather than Israel, for their plight. Had Israel obeyed the UN partition resolution it would have had internationally recognised borders and full UN support. The Arabs would then be in conflict with the UN, not with Israel. By staying within the UN borders and by maintaining a neutral policy towards the Palestinians and the Arab states Israel could have created a political climate in which a peace treaty with the Palestinians and other Arab states would have been possible. However, Ben-Gurion believed that King Abdallah would sign a peace treaty with him, thus putting to an end the separate (political) existence of the Palestinians.

Instead, a Palestinian Arab shot and killed Abdallah in the Al-Aqsa mosque in Jerusalem in 1951 and Israel found itself without peace, without internationally recognised borders, in conflict with the UN (for violating the partition resolution) and at war with the Palestinian Arabs who demanded their part of Palestine according to the UN resolution. It is quite possible that the conflict could have come to an end long ago had Ben-Gurion stayed within the UN partition resolution borders.

Another opportunity to end the conflict occurred in 1956 after President Nasser of Egypt nationalised the Suez Canal. Britain and

France prepared a military expedition to topple Nasser and repossess the canal but needed a pretext to attack Egypt. They signed a secret pact with Israel. According to this pact Israel would invade the Sinai peninsula and rush to the Suez Canal. The British-French armies would then occupy both banks of the canal, pretending to 'separate the adversaries' and 'guarantee free passage for international shipping through the canal'. Nasser knew of the plan and offered Ben-Gurion a peace treaty to forestall the Israeli attack. Ben-Gurion rejected the offer. He wanted Nasser to be toppled, enabling Israel to annex the Sinai peninsula with the blessing of Britain and France. As it happened, the USA, which was not party to this plot, forced Britain, France and Israel to withdraw. Nasser remained in power, the Prime Ministers of Britain and France, Anthony Eden and Guy Molet, had to resign, and Israel had to hand back the Sinai to Egypt. Ben-Gurion preferred a military adventurist policy in collusion with Britain and France to Nasser's peace offer. It is reasonable to assume that given Nasser's tremendous popularity in the Arab world, a peace treaty signed with him would have been accepted and endorsed by most Arab states, and by the Palestinians.

Another chance for peace was wasted by Israel after its victory in the 1967 war. In that war Israel conquered the whole of Palestine, plus the Sinai peninsula, and a great part of the Syrian 'Golan Heights'. Had Israel shown magnanimity after this victory, and offered to hand back most of the Sinai to Egypt and most of the Golan to Syria, while offering the West Bank and Gaza to the Palestinians to set up their state, it could have received in return a genuine peace with all these parties. Instead, Moshe Dayan, Israel's Defence Minister, who before the war had said 'we do not covet a single inch of Arab soil, we seek only to remove the sword threatening us', now declared that 'Sharem-el-Sheikh without peace is preferable to peace without Sharem-el-Sheikh' (Sharem-el-Sheikh is in the southern tip of the Sinai peninsula). Dayan also added that he was 'waiting for a telephone call from King Hussein of Jordan, to start negotiations for peace'. In other words, Israel refused to take any initiative towards a conciliatory policy seeking peace with the Arab world.

After 1967 Israel was intoxicated with its swift victory over the Arab states and began to believe it could play the role of a major power able to dominate the Middle East. It was clear that Egypt, Syria and the Palestinians would fight again to get their lands back. A future war became inevitable.

Why did the leadership of the Israeli labour movement, which led the Jewish community in Palestine from 1922 to 1977, reject every occasion for negotiating a settlement of the conflict in Palestine? Until 1948 the answer is simple: as long as the Jews were a minority in Palestine an agreement with the Palestinians could be reached only if it accepted the Arab demand to independence in the whole of Palestine. This would have meant an Arab state with a Jewish minority, in other words, the end of the Zionist project. A Jewish state in Palestine with an Arab majority implied minority rule, as in South Africa, where a white minority ruled a black majority. Ben-Gurion abhorred this and insisted that Jews must first become a majority through immigration and only afterwards demand independence. When he realised that Jews might remain a minority in Palestine he accepted the partition of the country, so that Jews would constitute a majority in part of the country. Zionism insisted there was no such thing as a Palestinian Arab people, only 'Arabs who happen to live in Palestine'. The reason was the right of nations to self-determination. Zionism based its own claim on this principle, and it therefore had to accept that if a Palestinian nation existed it deserved independence on its territory, thus negating the Zionist aim. For that reason Zionism always insisted that there is no such thing as a Palestinian people and that there must never be a Palestinian state in Palestine. Zionism saw any acceptance of political rights of the Palestinians in Palestine as a direct challenge to its own legitimacy.

This remains true even after the Israeli-PLO agreement of 1993. The agreement is quite clear on this point: no Palestinian state west of the River Jordan. If the Palestinians want a state, they can have it east of the River Jordan. No wonder the Hashemite rulers east of the Jordan are not enchanted by this possibility. Rabin's insistence on this point is direct continuation of Ben-Gurion's policy.

After 1948 another, hidden, reason for Ben-Gurion's rejection of any concilliatory policy towards the Arabs emerged. He was thinking not only of territorial gains but also of the social cohesion of the various Jewish communities in Israel. He was well aware that oriental Jews share a culture close to the Arabs and differ, culturally, from Western Jews. He feared a social-cultural conflict between oriental and European Jews in Israel. The fact that European Jews constitute the technological elite running Israel whereas the oriental Jews provide mostly unskilled manpower exacerbates the situation. Ben-Gurion figured that a situation of hostility with the Arabs would force the oriental Jews to accept Westernisation. He shaped the Israeli Army to serve as the major instrument for integrating the two communities by giving the oriental Jews an opportunity to prove their worth to the state, and to society, and to acquire, in the Army, modern Western skills. The ongoing hostility with the Arabs, and the frequent wars against them, turned the Army into the central institution in Israel, whose influence on the individual overrides the influence exerted by the family, or the school. Ben-Gurion did not want an active military conflict. He was neither a warmonger nor a militarist but he was not keen on reconciliation with the Arabs. Hostility without direct military confrontation suited him best. He never put forward a single idea for reconciliation and peace with the Palestinian people or with any Arab regime that was not under the influence of the West. He feared progress in the Arab world, like improvement of education and health facilities there, and above all he feared the possibility of a political unification of the Arab world. His disciples Eshkol, Golda Meir, Rabin, Peres, followed this policy.

No offers of peace have been made by Israel; no concessions were offered to the Arabs. Only the defeat in the 1973 war, and the political onslaught by President Sadat of Egypt and President Carter of the USA forced Israel to hand back the Sinai peninsula to Egypt. Why, then, did Rabin and Peres agree to hand back the Gaza strip and Jericho to the PLO?

Two reasons: first, the Intifada; second, the massive acquisition of rockets by Arab regimes.

In 1987 the Palestinian population in the occupied territories started an unarmed struggle against the Israeli occupation. In response Israeli soldiers shot dead, over a period of six years, 1,083 civilians, of whom 282 were under the age of 16. Eventually, most Israelis clamoured for an evacuation of the Gaza strip. Even M. Arens, the hawkish Minister of Defence in the nationalistic Likud Cabinet, proposed this evacuation, but Prime Minister Shamir, who has an ideological fixation on the entire territory west of the Jordan, refused to concede an inch. This caused the defeat of the Likud in the 1992 elections. Six years of ongoing unarmed resistance by the Palestinian civilian population convinced a majority of Israelis that the Palestinian people exist and have political demands for independence in Palestine. It also became clear in the long, futile negotiations in Madrid and Washington that neither Syria nor Jordan would sign a peace treaty with Israel before it reached an agreement with the Palestinians. This meant that another war with Arab states could occur if the Labour government failed to reach agreement with the Palestinians. However, remembering the Gulf War, when a few dozen Iraqi rockets caused mass panic in Israel, it became clear that the next war would bring a rain of rockets on the Israeli civilian population. The Rabin Cabinet decided to avert this possibility. To do so it had to negotiate with someone accepted by most Palestinians as their representative. This 'someone' was the PLO whom the entire Israeli leadership and media had demonised for decades as blood thirsty murderers. This demonisation was a direct result of the Zionist refusal to accept as legitimate any Palestinian claim for independence west of the Jordan. Since the Palestinians kept fighting, their struggle was described in criminal rather than political terms. Israel was not unique in this; the South African government denied for decades any political status to the ANC, and Britain refuses to grant the IRA political legitimacy. As a result all armed activities of these organisations are described in the media as devoid of any political context. The only context in which armed struggle, including killing, can then be placed is the criminal one. Thus did the PLO people become bloodthirsty murderers who kill Israelis only because of their Jewish origin. When Rabin and Peres realised that they could not quell the Palestinians in the occupied territories, most of whom support the PLO, and that the PLO, financially bankrupt, would lose credibility to Islamic groups because of its acceptance of the two-state solution, they decided to negotiate directly with the 'murderous' PLO rather than face the alternative. Peres said in an interview, 'One of my friends, a writer, warned me that the PLO has reached a point of such weakness that it might disappear from the map. I asked myself what will happen after the PLO disappears, what will replace it?'[2] The answer to that question is clear: the only organisations capable of replacing the PLO are the Islamic groups, financed by Iran, who fight for the creation of an Islamic republic in the whole of Palestine. With such groups no negotiations are possible and the only outcome is a new war. This realisation forced Rabin to throw a lifeline to the PLO and save it from political and financial bankruptcy. In return the PLO agreed to sign an agreement with Israel.

The handshake between Rabin and Arafat on the White House lawn on 13 September was a traumatic experience for most Israelis. They had to accept that the abominable PLO and Arafat are legitimate representatives of the Palestinian people. They had to accept that most of the West Bank will, eventually, be handed back to the Palestinians. However, the agreement signed in Washington does not allow the Palestinians to have their own currency, army or foreign policy. The Palestinians are allowed to run their internal affairs, thus relieving the Israelis of the task of policing them, but they are not allowed to create a genuinely independent state. The Israeli settlements in the occupied territories will not be dismantled and the Israeli Army, rather than the Palestinian police, will be responsible for their security. The Israeli Army will pull out of Arab-populated areas but will maintain a presence in the occupied territories. The agreement says nothing about the one and a half million Palestinian refugees of 1948 who live outside Palestine.

No wonder that many Palestinians, including PLO members, reject this agreement. As the agreement stands it means that the PLO will be allowed to administrate a kind of a Bantustan. Rabin keeps declaring that he will not allow a Palestinian state west of the Jordan. Advocates of the agreement argue that quite apart from the letter of this accord it shifts the course of Israeli–Arab relations from military confrontation to economic co-operation, and could start a process that will achieve full statehood for the

Palestinians. This brings to mind a comment by Friedrich Engels that 'history (and politics) is the realm of intentional action and unintentional outcome'. Political actions must be judged by intentions as well as by their outcome. Even if the Rabin-Arafat accord ushers in an era of economic co-operation and Palestinian independence, those who signed this accord must be judged first and foremost by their intentions. The intention of the Israeli leadership was, and remains, the central Zionist intention: to maintain, and strengthen, a state in Palestine which grants social and legal privileges to Jews. A non-Zionist Israel, accepting the Palestinians as equals, without discrimination, is not on. Genuine Palestinian independence west of the Jordan is not on. With this intention intact further conflict with the Palestinians and with the Arab world is lurking in the future.

Notes and References

1. *Collected Works of Ahad-Ha'am* (Hebrew), 1950, Jerusalem: Dvir, p. 24.
2. *Yediot Haronot*, 15 September 1993.

Index

Abdallah, King, of Trans-Jordan, 79, 165
'accomplished facts', mentality of settlers generation, 35, 37
adaptation, and cultural identity, 11, 15, 61–2, see also assimilation
Agranat, Justice, Appeal Court judge, 109–11
Agudat Israel (The Jewish Association), 20
Ahad-Ha'am (Asher Ginzburg), 30, 41; foresees Palestinian conflict, 161–2, 164; 'Political Zionism – The Jewish State and the Jewish Problem', 162–4
Aloni, Ms Shulamit, Minister of Education, 44, 48
America see United States of America
American Indians, 64
Americanisation, in Israel, 55
Americans, black, 124
Amish, and traditional culture, 61, 154
anthropocentricity, of Christianity, 14, 120–1; of socialism, 120, 142–3, 150, see also humanism
anti-semitism, anti-Zionism as, 24, 25–7; Zionism dependent on, 30, see also discrimination, anti-Jewish
anti-Zionist left in Israel, and Palestinian proposal for Jewish-Arab state, 127–9

Arab society, nature of, 60–1, 135–7, see also Mashreq
Arab-Israeli conflict, analysis of, 5–6, 79, 137; peace negotiations (1993), 49, see also Palestine; Palestinians
Arabs, Israeli view of, 22–3, 79, 162
Arafat, Yasser, at United Nations (1974), 127; and recognition of PLO, 160, 169
Arens, M., 168
Arrow-Cross (Hungarian fascists), 84–5, 100
assimilation, and cultural identity, 11, 15, 30, 61; Zionism as failed, 30, 160, see also adaptation; Zionism
atheism, as contradiction of Jewishness, 62–3; of Israeliness, 46–7
Auschwitz, Eichmann's deportation of Jews to, 84, 85; Kastner's knowledge of, 90, 93; schoolchildren's views of, 48–9; Vrba's report on, 86–8
Avishar, Leeran (schoolboy), 48, 49
Avriel, Ehud, Jewish Agency, 115

Bagdhad, Israeli bombing of (1948), 6
bar mitzvah ceremony, 10, 13, 14

Pluto Middle Eastern Studies

Jewish History, Jewish Religion

The Weight of Three Thousand Years

Israel Shahak

Foreword by Gore Vidal

'Shahak is an outstanding scholar, with remarkable insight
and depth of knowledge. His work is informed and
penetrating, a contribution of great value.'
Noam Chomsky

'The voice of reason is alive and well, and in Israel, of all
places. Like a highly learned Thomas Paine, Shahak
illustrates the prospect before us, as well as the long history
behind us, and thus he continues to reason. He is the latest
– if not the last – of the great prophets.'
Gore Vidal

Written from a humanitarian viewpoint by a Jewish scholar,
this is a rare and highly controversial criticism of Israel that
will both excite and disturb readers. The book is an English
language original and addressed to readers living outside
the state of Israel.

ISBN hardback: 0 7453 0818 X softback: 0 7453 0819 8

Order from your local bookseller or contact the publisher on
081 348 2724.

Pluto Press
345 Archway Road, London N6 5AA
5500 Central Avenue, Boulder, Colorado 80301, USA

Published by Pluto Press

Original Sins
Reflections on the History of Zionism and Israel

Benjamin Beit-Hallahmi

Starting from a non-idealising, non-demonological review of Judaism, Jewish history and anti-Semitism, this book presents a sympathetic analysis of the development of political Zionism. Beit-Hallahmi shows how Zionism in practice becomes settler colonialism, trying to ignore its victims – the Palestinians.

Published 1991 ISBN softback: 0 7453 0514 8

Perdition: A Play in Two Acts
Jim Allen

'The core of the play is the exposure of real facts, commonly distorted or unduly denied by the pervading Zionist propaganda.' *Maxine Rodinson, Director-École Pratique des Hautes Études, Sorbonne*

The complete text of the controversial play plus notes by Lenni Brenner and Akiva Orr, who attended the Kastner trial on which the play is based.

Published 1990   ISBN softback: 0 86372 100 1

Order from your local bookseller or contact the publisher on 081 348 2724.

Pluto Press
345 Archway Road, London N6 5AA